The Last Testament

The Last Testament

Don Cupitt

scm press

© Don Cupitt 2012

Published in 2012 by SCM Press
Editorial office
3rd Floor, Invicta House,
108-114 Golden Lane,
London, EC1Y 0TG, UK

SCM Press is an imprint of Hymns Ancient & Modern Ltd
(a registered charity)
13A Hellesdon Park Road
Norwich NR6 5DR, UK

www.scmpress.co.uk

British Library Cataloguing in Publication data

A catalogue record for this book is available
from the British Library

978-0-334-04622-6
Kindle edition 978-0-334-04623-3

Originated by The Manila Typesetting Company
Printed and bound by
CPI Group (UK) Ltd, Croydon, CR0 4YY

Contents

☆ Jesus reconstructed. ✓ by the early church

Preface

In New Testament times and for long afterwards – perhaps even until the late twentieth century – many or most people saw this present life of ours as preparatory. They hoped for a better here-after, perhaps after death in the case of the individual, or in the long-term historical future on earth, in the case of the human race as a whole.

Today we have lost those old hopes. We seem to regard our funerary rites as simply giving closure to the individual life. Nobody sees funerals as occasions for serious repentance in the face of impending divine Judgement. As for the communal hopes, whether religious, or liberal, or anarchist, or socialist, it seems today that we'll be lucky if we can achieve long-term sustainability by strictly controlling population and consumption. Progress is dead.

Either way, it seems that from now on we must learn to see this present life in the present social world as being our last. Our present human life-world is not being orchestrated towards a long-awaited climax and fulfilment. On the contrary, it is end-less and outside-less. It goes on and on like a soap opera, but we'll never arrive at anything radically different. It goes on, but it's not going anywhere special. Nor are we.

If that is so – and I am sure that it is – the question arises of whether the traditional goals of religion are 'immanently attainable': that is, they can be realized now, and within this life. Can we achieve a state of eternal happiness or blessedness in the here and now? In the past both Christians and Buddhists have held that it is indeed possible for a few exceptional saints to reach Enlightenment, or the Vision of God, within their own lifetimes, but might it ever be possible to *democratize* that idea within a future religion of ordinary life?

What are we asking for? I think few people doubt that it is possible to be enraptured by art, by the beauty of the natural world, and by what people call 'the joys of life'. But we need also to find a way of reconciling ourselves to life's transience, a way of persuading human beings to get on with each other better, and a way of seeing this world as a satisfactory theatre for effective moral action.

For years I have been trying to spell out an answer to this question about a secular religion that really works and can reach the heights; an answer that will satisfy not only me, but some others too. The best I have done may be found in two very short books, the *Solar Ethics* of 1995, and *The Fountain* of 2011. In this book I try to go a stage further, by arguing that our modern science-based industrial, and now globalized, civilization is so different from anything that came before it that it forces us to move on spiritually by a whole dispensation. In terms of Christian theology, this means that we must move on from the age of the Church (an age in which people saw this present world as penultimate) to the promised age of the Kingdom of God on earth (an age in which people can see their present life as being their last). Along these lines we may be able to show that the secular religion we need can be created out of what remains of Christianity – and is indeed the old faith's long-awaited fulfilment.

This seemingly odd suggestion turns out surprisingly effective. It prompts us to think that religion all along, and ever since its remote beginnings, was a way of reconciling ourselves to life and to each other. Belief in a spirit-world and in life after death was needed in the past, because it helped to make life intelligible and bearable in times when most people's lives were short, uncertain and harsh. But today the enormous development of modern knowledge, and of the technologies of modern medicine, communications and so on, have done much to make us less dependent upon the protection of a postulated supernatural order. More than the people of any previous period, we have come to ourselves and are able simply to love life just as it is.

In Part 1 of *The Last Testament* are some short essays that attempt to bend some traditional Christian ideas into the required new shapes. The new ideas presented are intended to be just true, and in a way that everyone already knows, so that I can claim no personal credit for them. I am only their 'presenter', or editor, and I formally disclaim any personal copyright in the text. I am determined to avoid the portentous pastiche biblical tone of the many writers who, since Nietzsche's *Zarathustra*, have attempted to write a new and updated version of the New Testament. (How could Nietzsche, of all people, have made such a mistake?) So these little essays are not scriptures, nor are they to be regarded as an individual's art product. They are meant to be the merest platitudes, and interesting chiefly for the way they show that nobody before now has ever really attempted to describe a religion that is simply *true*, with no mystique of the Catholic type that is designed to bamboozle the poor punters. In religion people ordinarily desire and expect to be overawed by tradition, by priestly power, by sheer size, and by illusory consolations. In short, by the Baroque. But here let us try if we can to persuade ourselves to be interested in the simple philosophical *truth* of the matter – and no more than that. Just religion, without self-deception.

In Part 2 of this book I present some public lectures, position statements written for various audiences during the past decade. They are occasional and personal, which is why I compare them with the canonical Epistles.

'A New Method of Religious Enquiry' – Chapter 10 – was written for the Highlands Institute in Highlands, North Carolina, and delivered on 26 September 2005.

'What's the Point of It All?' – Chapter 11 – began as a Summer School lecture at Cambridge in 2004, and was subsequently published in the journal *Arts and Humanities in Higher Education*, Vol. 4(2), pp.149–58 (2005).

'On the Meaning of Life' – Chapter 12 – was a public lecture for the University of Leuven, Belgium in March 2004.

'What's Happening to Religion?' – Chapter 13 – was written for the First National Conference of Sea of Faith in Australia and delivered at Wollaston College, Claremont, near Perth WA, in September 2004.

'The Religion of Ordinary Life' – Chapter 14 – quotes a systematic summary from *Above Us Only Sky* (Santa Rosa, CA: Polebridge Press, 2008). In the form reprinted here, it was delivered in various places – including Steyning, Sussex – during the next 18 months.

'The Ethics of Value-Creation' – Chapter 15 – was written as one of the annual Sea of Faith lectures I used to give at the National Conference which is held each year in Leicester, UK. This one dates from July 2005.

All these pieces are, I suppose, exercises in popular communication because they have to be. I don't believe in any revelation or special supernatural communication of religious truth, and I reject many other associated ideas. For example, it used to be held that the most important kind of religious truth is beyond the scope of unassisted human reason. It has been specially communicated to us by God, *via* an angel, to a prophet who has written it down in a holy book. The religious community guards the book and its officers teach the correct interpretation of it – and so on. Today I don't believe a word of all that. In the Last World, today's world, religious truth is in fact obvious, and freely available to everyone. In a sense, you already know it perfectly well. My job is only to use philosophical method, and various forms of popular communication, to try to bring real religious truth imaginatively to life. *Your* life. I have to try to persuade you to give up a lot of old and outworn ways of thinking so that you can learn a new, secular, everyday way to religious happiness. You know it all already, but I have to try to give an extra shove.

I have made five or six attempts to write a last book, but they all turned out unsuccessful, so I make no further such promise here. Thanks again to Linda Allen.

Cambridge, January 2012   D. C.

PART ONE

The Gospel

I

Dispensations

A restaurant that has recently changed hands bears a freshly painted sign saying UNDER NEW MANAGEMENT, and we are to understand that under the new regime everything is somewhat different. The whole atmosphere of the place is changed: by implication, for the better.

Rather similarly, when a new Master arrives at a College, he or she may bustle about, making an impression, changing things; and with the very mildest-possible irony the older Fellows in their armchairs will slightly raise, rather than actually *roll*, their eyes as they refer to 'the new dispensation'.

A dispensation, in this latter use, is a comprehensive regime both of truth and of practices that prevails in a society over a long period. Other terms are sometimes used: world-age, epoch, *aiōn/eon*, and the rather less emphatic 'period'.

The earlier uses of 'dispensation' were usually theological, and both Christianity and Islam need the idea, for they are both faiths that presuppose at least one earlier, preparatory religious order. In Christianity there are obviously at least two dispensations, the Old Testament (or Covenant) and the New, BC and AD. Closer examination increases the number to at least five: the world-ages of Innocence (Eden), the Patriarchs (Abraham), the Law of Moses, the Church (or, the Gospel), and the future Messianic Kingdom. World history is seen as a cosmic drama of Fall and Redemption planned by God, and by him ordered in a progressive series of distinct acts or stages. Each stage has its own characteristic ways of thinking and of doing things; its distinctive theology, ritual and ethics. Sometimes they are portrayed as so many different stages

3

in God's progressive self-revelation, and in the religious education of humankind.

Today, when Christianity is a largely forgotten religion, people may be unaware of it, but theology really is notably different in the different dispensations. In Eden, God is very anthropomorphic. He looks, and he talks to Adam, like a man who 'walks in the garden in the cool of the day'. In the Law, God is firmly One, very definitely spirit and not flesh, highly exalted but still *monocultural*: God's language is classical Hebrew, and he is covenanted exclusively to the Jews. He is *their* God, and very jealous about it. In the Gospel, God is Triune, multicultural and now firmly wedded to dispensationalism. He has become the God of *all* the descendants of Adam, and not only of the children of Abraham. Finally, in the Kingdom (or 'Heaven') God is dispersed. He is an intellectual 'brightness' that irradiates everything, with no remaining shadows or darkness at all, and his reality is no longer 'focused' at any ritual Centre or temple. 'Organized religion' is no longer needed.

Ideas of God, then, are dispensationally relative. Because the Bible and the classical theologians, especially in the Latin tradition and especially between Paul and Calvin, are so conscious of deep historical change in religion, they would seem to be committed to the view that there is no strictly immutable dogmatic truth. Take for example the Patriarchal period, between the Flood and the Exodus. It seems to be a distinct dispensation, because a great Patriarch like Abraham can apparently have any number of wives and concubines, and can build an altar and perform his own sacrifices without any need for the ministry of a priest, such as in later periods was needed to act on his behalf.

Anomalies like this could scarcely escape the notice of classical theologians, but they did not find them easy to resolve. How do you prevent conflict between the ideas of History and Truth? The fact is that in the three traditions of Abrahamic faith (Judaism, Christianity and Islam) it has always been very difficult to reconcile the acknowledged facts of deep historical change with the religious authorities' claim to have been entrusted with a body of immutable Truth revealed by a changeless and supremely real

Being. People seem to insist upon regarding their own religious order as permanent and immutable, even though they know it had a beginning and that a successor to it is promised.

Nor are all these arguments entirely obsolete. Thomas Kuhn's book *The Structure of Scientific Revolutions* (1962) led to parallel controversies about the history of science. In general physical theory and cosmology there have in the West been three main periods: first, there was the long period of classical natural philosophy presided over by such figures as Aristotle and Ptolemy; secondly, there was the period of mechanistic and eventually Newtonian physics that was opened by Galileo and Descartes, and which after Newton enjoyed cultural supremacy during the eighteenth and nineteenth centuries; and thirdly, there is today's physics, inaugurated by Einstein's papers on relativity and sealed by the development of quantum mechanics. These three great periods in the history of physics are rather like dispensations in theology. Kuhn calls them paradigms. As in religion some great event or deed is needed to bring about a change of dispensation, so in science it takes a figure of genius to see that a long-established paradigm, or set of framework assumptions, no longer works very well and needs to be replaced. Most of the time, scientific work is routine business and there is no felt need to question generally held assumptions that are working well enough. But now and again somebody comes along who by an enormous intellectual effort succeeds in putting the accepted paradigm seriously in question, and then goes on to suggest how a completely new set of ideas might work better.

Such a major change of paradigm is an uncommon but intellectually very exciting event. Kuhn called it a paradigm shift. But it is important to remember that in the case of physics, the older paradigm 'saved the phenomena' in its day. It covered the known facts. It was compatible with people's observations, and it may well have become so embedded in ordinary language that we still refer constantly to it. For example, in ordinary language we still refer to sunrise and sunset as if we still believe in the old geocentric world-picture; and we still in both everyday life and everyday engineering happily continue to use Newtonian ideas of matter and motion, space and time and so on. In both cases, the old ways of thinking still seem to fit the observed facts and to work well enough in practice. The fact that we now do this has helped to spread a pragmatist view of truth among philosophers and scientists.

Thus it seems that both in theology and in physics we can and must acknowledge that truth is paradigm-relative. In both cases, too, we can and do sometimes drop back with pleasure into the language of a now-superseded paradigm, especially in areas where the older ways still fit the observed facts, still generate accurate predictions, and (like 'sunset') still have their ancient poetic appeal to us. By the same token, I still sometimes catch myself praying. I shouldn't do it, but I do.

The parallel between dispensations in the history of religion and paradigms in the history of science is also important to us in another way. We want to argue that the 'years of Grace', the long years of Church-Christianity, are now over. Even in the Reformation period, various of the would-be Reformers were already arguing that the Church period was now ended, and that it was time to make the move to the next dispensation, the Messianic Kingdom. This urge to move on by a whole epoch had some interesting political outcomes: one was our modern liberal democracy; another, the dream that is America. Of its religious products, the Radical Reformation's most lastingly important creation and survival is the Society of Friends, the 'Quakers', who – in England at least – have clearly left behind them the Church and its dogmatic theology and are attempting to live the next dispensation, the Kingdom of God on earth.

The claim that the Church had become obsolete had another consequence. It prompted attempts to reform and renew Church-Christianity, attempts which gave us the Baroque Catholicism of the Counter-Reformation, Evangelical Protestantism, and so on. But there has also been a growing realization that the main objection to the old faith is that its theology is now known to be untrue. Intellectuals have had serious philosophical doubts and scriptural doubts for several centuries. Perhaps the most persuasive is the fact that the New Testament does not actually teach orthodox doctrine. The main body of middle-class literary folk came to their crisis of faith during the 1840s. By the late nineteenth century unbelieving theologians were becoming common. In Edwardian times the Cambridge faculty was notoriously sceptical. Today many church historians suggest that among ordinary people 'the death of Christian Britain' happened in the 1960s. Today, even in the USA, two thirds of 'Generation Y' (the 18–30 age group) are completely unchurched.

Church-Christianity is now in headlong and terminal decline. Its whole exegesis of the Bible, and its whole supernaturalist worldview – based upon belief in God, in supernatural causes of events, and in life after death – is dead. For all practical purposes we all now think that there is for us only one life in one world, and it is *this* world, the ordinary human life-world. In short, we are now in the last world we'll ever know, and all ideas of a greater reality beyond the horizon of this life have perished. If nevertheless they remain permanently religious, people may mark the change by saying that they prefer to describe themselves as 'spiritual'.

The position of the Church really is, literally, *terminal*. In that case, a theologian may suggest that we should now regard the entire theology of Church-Christianity as being religiously and historically obsolete. A change of dispensation is occurring, and we should see ourselves as entering the Kingdom period. We should remember that according to the ancient Biblical promise, the Kingdom of God on earth was to be – like our life-world – the *last* world, the world with no further world beyond it, a secular and humanistic world in which at last human beings are fully reconciled to each other and to life. Not a world with no evil, certainly, but a world in which we really do start living the ethics of the original Jesus, who is now seen as having been simply a human teacher.

The old promise seems now to be our fact: and the principle that 'religious truth is dispensationally relative' gives us all the scope we need for a major reinvention of our tradition. We can shake it up like a kaleidoscope, and see what new pattern it falls into.

To this, many will object that dispensationalism is itself a complex *supernaturalist* theology of history. We cannot appeal to it in support of a radically secularized one-world theology. Of all the

Grand Narrative myths that we have finally lost in modern times, the most important was precisely that ancient belief that the whole of human history can be recounted as a long march through many religiously different stages, towards a final liberation of all humankind. We cannot simultaneously appeal to such ideas, *and* purport to transcend them.

However, nobody has accused T. S. Kuhn of having put forward a supernaturalist, or even necessarily a *progressivist*, theory of the history of science. He is simply making a distinction between times when scientific research plods on quietly within a generally accepted paradigm set of assumptions, and great and exciting periods of revolutionary change when a whole big branch of science is in process of being rethought. Kuhn's theory is secular, and today many physicists are ready to discuss whether certain recent reports and developments indicate that we have to consider the possibility that a new paradigm shift may be needed, and may be coming. Thus Kuhn's theory may already be doing a good job by encouraging modern physicists to read the signs of their own times, and to diagnose the way their subject is going.

This parallel suggests that if we say that the Church and its ancient supernatural theology are finished, and that we need to move on to build a Kingdom theology for our own secular humanist culture, we are not making a bad intellectual error by simultaneously invoking, and promising deliverance from, the old theology of history as a great salvation drama written and now being staged by God. No, it's just a human fact that as culture develops corresponding religious change is sure to follow. Today, cultural globalization is proceeding apace, stimulated by the very rapid growth of cheap, fast and high-capacity communications and information storage and retrieval. The old local and traditional roots from which the main religions used to draw their authority are now a handicap. The new media are detraditionalizing us very fast indeed, and if religious thought and feeling are to have any future at all, some at least of us need to start rethinking everything in the new conditions.

2

The Fountain

When people talk about 'the creation of the world' they usually have in mind a moment in the past when the Universe suddenly exploded into existence. In our physical cosmology this moment is currently dated about 13.5 billion years ago. When religious people hear about this, they are tempted to ask: 'But what was there *before* the Big Bang? Why did it occur?' – and the questioner seems to be hoping to hear that God was around before the Big Bang, and that he caused it to occur by a sudden, one-off act of his creative Will.

At this point, the argument may go off in two different directions. The scientists will probably want to say that the 'Initial Singularity' is a limit towards which our present picture of the Universe points back, very much as the lines of longitude on the terrestrial globe all lead up to and converge at the North Pole. Asking what *caused* the Big Bang to occur, and talking about a time *before* the Big Bang is meaningless. It makes the same mistake as asking 'What is there that is to the North of the North Pole?' The North Pole is the limit of northernness. From it all roads go only South. Similarly, there is no sense in talking about a time before time began. As for the *existence* of the Universe, as I understand it that nowadays is simply a matter of probabilities. Even at Absolute Zero °K in a vacuum, there is a constant spitter and spatter of particles of matter and antimatter popping into existence and popping out of it again. These events are called 'quantum fluctuations'. But notice that they violate the traditional maxim in metaphysics, *Ex nihilo nihil fit* (Out of nothing, nothing can come). So there is no longer a sharp dividing line between what exists and what does not exist. Arguments to the effect that in order to exist at all the world needs a World Ground or First Cause which is timelessly and absolutely Real have thus suddenly come to appear obsolete.

That's the way that the scientists will want to conduct the argument. What about the philosophers? Until the early eighteenth century most of the leading philosophers believed in God, and they had done so since late classical antiquity. But in the old theistic metaphysics God's creation of the world was not a one-off event, as if God at the very beginning had somehow magicked the world into existence, and thereafter had left it alone, apart from intervening in emergencies. On the contrary, the standard doctrine was that the entire Universe, every bit of it and every event in it, was *continuously* kept in be-ing by the creative Will of God. Only God was self-existent, or 'necessarily existent', as they put it. Creatures are only contingently in existence *just now*, and they can continue in being only for so long as God chooses to preserve them. According to the old metaphysics, God minus the world equals God, because God is entirely self-sufficient and perfect, and doesn't need the world at all; but the world minus God equals nothing. Its relation to God is constitutive of the creature's very existence, all the time. If there is no God, there can be no world – and of course no substantial self, or soul, either.

So much for the old philosophy of God. It raises two points of interest. First, it was *already* aware that finite, contingent being is temporal. The world cannot just stay in being by itself. Somehow, it needs to be kept going, or be upheld, all the time. Be-ing, with a hyphen, seems to be something like a process, a sustained activity in time. Secondly, during the eighteenth century the work of Hume and Kant demolished the traditional metaphysics of God. As Kant grew old, around the year 1800, the first really confident modern philosophies *after God* were being written in Germany by people such as Fichte, Schelling and Schopenhauer. Hegel and Kierkegaard, in their different ways, tried to cause diversions and to delay the inevitable, but the fact is that since about 1800 no major philosopher has been a straightforward theist of the traditional kind. The Death of God happened during the later eighteenth century, and nobody is going to turn the clock back now. We are on our own – *and the world is on its own, too*: it is unsustained.

Suddenly, we see a question. If it is not upheld in being all the time by the creative Will of God, how does the world manage to continue in being *at all*? Surely the Death of God must entail the death of the world and of the self as well? Doesn't the Death of God lead at once to pure nihilism? Or alternatively, how does finite being continue in being? Don't ask: *Did God cause the First Event*? Ask instead: *What continuously supports all finite beings and maintains them in being*? At the very least, the great intellectual event that people call 'the Death of God' calls for a new ontology, or theory of be-ing.

Modern philosophy has given various answers to this question. Much of German Idealist philosophy advises us to give up talking of the world as independently real, apart from us. The world is *our* world, real *for us* within and through our knowledge of it. Linguistic philosophy goes a little further, and sees the world as constructed by our language, and as real only in our theorizing of it and our debates about it. In approximately the same vein, Nietzsche says: 'There are no facts, only interpretations.' But what do we interpret? Nietzsche suggests that the ultimate constituents of the world are tiny forces or energies. The rest is human interpretation, as we struggle briefly to impose human pattern and meaning upon the white noise of experience. Heidegger suggests that we need to go back to the beginnings of Western thought, and completely rethink our ideas about Be-ing. In particular, we need to give up the old assumption that the most Real kind of being is timeless, and instead we should start from the newer understanding that all being is temporal. All being is by a continuous outpouring of be-ing, hyphenated, which is not a thing but a process.

How might we envisage this process? In Jay Jopling's White Cube gallery in London I once saw an interesting Damien Hirst sculpture. It was a white skeleton, lying flat on a clear plastic horizontal Cross, a standard representation of Christ's death as a state of nothingness that awaits us all. But by the head of the skeleton

Hirst had set a hairdryer, wired up and switched on. On the up-rushing column of air was balanced a table tennis ball. It danced a little, suggesting that finite being is kept in be-ing by a continuous invisible uprush from out of the Nothingness that Hirst connects imaginatively with the dead Christ.

Works of art like Damien Hirst's have led me to think that it may be possible to replace the traditional metaphysics of God with a new kind of 'poetical' religious and philosophical thinking which sees life under one or more great unifying and reconciling symbols. I want images of an outpouring silent process that pours out and passes away all the time. It has no metaphysical Ground. It is perpetually self-renewing. And it isn't 'going anywhere': it's going everywhere – scattering and dying away.

Four main images of this outpouring have suggested themselves to me during the last seventeen years or so – Life, Fire, the Sun, and the Fountain. Each of them seems perpetually to renew it-self. Coming from nowhere, it wells up apparently spontaneously. Coming out into public expression, it flowers and then immedi-ately passes away. All these images seem to meet in the image of *broadcasting*. The sower broadcasts the seed with sweeping gestures that scatter it over the earth, and he moves on without pausing to check how effective his action is. His job is only to publish and pass on, heedlessly. That's his thing: it's what he does. And much the same may be said of today's torrent of hu-man communication.

A recent book called *The Fountain* begins by remarking that during the past 30 years we have lived through an enormously rapid growth of cheap worldwide communications and informa-tion technology, leading to very rapid social and cultural change. We have become acutely aware of transience and of our own mutability. Above all, we are haunted by the knowledge of our own mortality. All the old philosophical, religious and ethical cer-tainties have melted away. Nothing is eternal: everything quickly becomes obsolete, including ourselves. It seems that our greatest religious need now is to be reconciled to universal transience.

The Fountain offers a purely rational poetical theology for this new era. It is an image that evokes, draws together and reconciles an extraordinarily wide range of phenomena: the continuous self-renewal of all be-ing, Big Bang cosmology in physics, the endless self-propagation of life itself when it finds a new habitat and fans out to fill it, and the self-renewal of our own life when we wake up each morning, when spring returns after a hard winter, when we experience the birth of our own children and grandchildren, and when we feel the urge to express ourselves and communicate with others. Imagery of outpouring and self-scattering is much used in religion, too: think of diaspora, dispersal and dissemination. In Christianity there is the breaking and the distribution of Christ's Body in the Eucharist, and the outpouring of God as Spirit at Pentecost. But behind these Christian themes there is also the larger religious and cultural theme of *democratization*: over the centuries powers and privileges that once belonged only to the gods have gradually become diffused through the whole of society. In the end everything gets disseminated or scattered. There are no firm and enduring identities. Everything passes away forever.

It is at this point that the Fountain image begins to affect ethics. Since about the 1880s, people have more and more come to see the moral life in expressive terms. The old Platonic spirituality of *introversion* had people withdrawing from society, and turning inwards to seek God in the depths of their own souls. The voice of conscience made itself heard in that solitary inwardness. But now people more and more want to come out of the closet and be themselves without any concealment, *in public*. Ideas of spontaneity, sincerity and authenticity have become very important in ethics. The word 'person' originally meant a mask, a role in a publicly performed drama, so that if modern people want above all the freedom to be fully themselves they will not queue up to enter convents and monasteries, but will seek instead to achieve and enact their selfhood in public space. The new outlook takes a notably theatrical view of the self as *persona*: 'The show', we say, 'must go on.' Everybody wants to come out and do his or her thing.

By now we are all familiar with the idea of body language, and with the related idea that you are making public statements all the time by the way you dress and present yourself. I pursue these ideas with the deliberate intention of reversing the whole direction of traditional religious life. Don't retreat into inwardness: go out and put on a good show! Burn, baby, burn! Present yourself! Do your thing! Sparkle, shine!

Why am I reversing the traditional spirituality? I'm doing it because until very recently it was generally believed that our present world is penultimate. It is a world in which we are under discipline, preparing ourselves for a promised better world that is yet to come. The better world might be thought of as located in Heaven, or it might be a future and far better state of life upon this earth. But however you thought of the better world, it was worthwhile to work hard at purifying yourself now, for the sake of a greater glory hereafter. You did without transient earthly pleasures for the sake of a promised eternal happiness in the world to come.

However, all such hopes have now collapsed. There is no life after death, no Paradise, and no post-revolutionary utopia that will come one day. This present world around us is *already* the last world we will ever know. Death is simple extinction, and we should not waste the only life we will ever have. We should not postpone the final ethic: we should hasten to live it now. We should live life to its fullest, and make the most of it while we have it. As the admirably brutal saying has it, **Get a life!**; or, just a little more kindly: **You should get out more.**

In parks and other public places, the Fountain is often situated at a place where many different ways meet. It is a focus, it attracts the eye, and so it is a unifying image. But more than that: the Fountain viewed close up is nothing but foaming, uprushing, formless contingency; but when we step back and look at it from a distance, it becomes soothing and peaceful, a symbol to meditate upon. It symbolizes calm, refreshment, healing, cleansing, and life's perpetual self-renewal. It helps to reconcile us not only to the transience of everything but, still more, to *our own* transience. Like the Fountain, we too live by expressing ourselves. We pour out, we communicate with others, we pass on and eventually we pass away – and how could it be otherwise? So the Fountain, as we gaze at it sparkling in the sunshine, may help us to say Amen to our own finite lives.

I am not quite saying that the Fountain is God. The Fountain is only a traditional religious symbol, often seen in public squares, in leisure gardens and in memorial gardens. It's only a metaphor, but along with other great religious symbols such as the Sun, the Fire, and Life, it may yet be able to do for us the sort of things that God used to do. Poetically, at least, religious thought and feeling are still possible after God.

Since about 1995, I've been calling this philosophy of mine 'Energetic Spinozism'. Like Spinoza himself, I want to teach a form of religious naturalism, 'a secular theology'. But whereas Spinoza's vision is strictly rational and even quasi-geometrical, speaking as it does of substance, of rational intuition, and of eternity, my own vision is influenced by Darwin and Freud, and I speak of an explosive outpouring of energies and e-motions that come out into expression in us and around us, and are read by us as signs. I'd like to be happy to burn, burn out and pass away. That's all there is for any of us, and I want to learn to say Amen to it. I'd rather be a mortal human than an immortal angel who doesn't know the bittersweetness of a human life in time. I'd rather seek religious happiness by coming out, briefly doing my thing, and passing away, than seek it by retiring from the world and from human history in order to live by anticipation the timeless life of Heaven.

So it is that in the past two decades I have been trying to turn religious thought inside out. I reject the old metaphysical kind of philosophy that we all learnt from Plato. I reject the old accounts of the division of reality into two distinct worlds – a transient visible world in which we live now, and a deep, unseen, eternal world to which we hope to proceed after death. Instead I say that there's no world but this human world. This is already the last world. So we should give up the whole idea of this life being a state of probation, in which we are preparing ourselves for Heaven after death. We give up the introvertive spirituality of turning within to find our 'real' immortal selves, and instead we come out, embracing the extravertive way, living life as intensely and affirmatively as we can while we are in it.

As it happens, this ethic is not new. There was someone who taught it in the ancient world.

3

Poetical Truth and Common Life

In Arnold Bennett's novel *The Old Wives' Tale* (1908, Part 1, c.4.1) occurs the following sentence:

She was left behind; and the joy of life was calling her.

The date is the late 1860s. Sophia Baines, aged about 15, is for the moment 'minding' the family business, a big draper's shop in the industrial town of Bursley, Staffordshire, England. The town's chief annual festival, its Wakes Week, is going on half a mile away, and Sophia suddenly, desperately, wants to be there and part of it. 'Life' is calling her, and no girl of her age is going to let life pass her by if she can help it.

So what is 'life'? It is one of the dozen most frequently used common nouns in the language, with an enormous range of modern meanings, uses and idioms. It is ordinary biological life; it is a kind of uprushing, streaming energy that powers our existence and keeps us continuously 'on the go'; it is therefore also *libido*, a continuous outpouring of often rather mixed and even conflicted emotion within us that strives to get out into expression, whether real or symbolic, and so it is therefore in the end the whole human life-world, a social world of continuous physical, economic and symbolic exchange. It is the news; it is history; it is 'what's on', and it is therefore the 'buzz' of the bright lights in city centres to which young people especially are irresistibly drawn.

We have scarcely begun yet! Life is always on the move. It flows and energizes, like blood, or water, or electricity. Life is the human world; life is the medium in which we all of us live and move and have our being, and our human life is above all the subject matter of the novel. During the early nineteenth century artists and writers at last began to discover and explore the 'culture', the life, and the world of ordinary people. The world is not governed, and history is not made, by the great alone, as had hitherto been generally assumed. There was a sudden *democratization* of thought that began to turn God into 'life', the sermon into the novel, and Providence into the *Zeitgeist*.

From early on there was a tendency to personify life, to see it as replacing the old God who was now in retreat, and to speak of it as being automobile – *self*-powered, or even 'turned on' by itself. Indeed, the joy of life, its exhilaration, is the ease and the speed of its self-enhancement. Particularly vivid is the case where two people on meeting may instantly 'hit it off'. There is 'chemistry' between them, as the idiom has it. In their encounter life recognizes itself, and in each of them the feeling of being alive, the *Lebensgefühl*, suddenly surges or is enhanced.

Especially since the mid-twentieth century, these ways of thinking about life have spread from the novelists who pioneered them through the idioms of our everyday speech. They are now entrenched, but you may well sharply object that mechanistic science knows nothing of a ubiquitous 'life force' that pervades the human life-world and powers each and every living being. Many of the new idioms sound to some people vitalistic in a thoroughly bad way.

I reply that there would indeed be a danger of vitalism, and also a risk of falling into extreme right-wing political ideology, if we were to understand the language of life too realistically. Jacques Derrida made the same point about the closely related language of spirit: *esprit de corps*, team spirit and so forth. We should insist that we are not talking any kind of science when we seem to speak of spirit as a powerful gas or breath, and of life as an intoxicating liquid flow. We are not talking science, and we are not talking strict philosophy, either. Rather, we are talking what we should describe as 'poetical' philosophy or theology. We are seeing life as a very pervasive and powerful unifying metaphor that helps us to link many different aspects of the 'flow' of things in the human life-world, in a post-metaphysical age. There are no substances: there are only trains of events. Life-talk helps us see the series of events as a *stream* that flows. William James introduced the phrase 'the stream of thought' for the same reason, for we do need to think of the self as living, developing and continuous. It is born, and it dies. In Platonism, the soul was commonly spoken of as being not only the principle of life – and as such, clearly part of the world of biological life, of time and change – but also as being an immortal spiritual substance whose true home is the eternal world. Thus Plato himself affirmed both the pre-existence of the soul *before* our earthly life in time, and also the continuation of the soul's life *after* death. But when we give up the metaphysics of substance, we can begin to see ourselves as coincident with and identical with our own finite lives in time. I am not a substance, I *am* my living of my own life, I am just a chain of events to which an identity is imputed – by society, by you, by myself. I am my own living of my own life. A Buddhist writer, hammering home the point, even says: 'I *am* time.' I am just a fictioned unifying interpretation of the streaming events of my own life.

If I fully accept all this, then I shall be freed from a number of traditional errors. I shall have to commit myself wholly to my own life. I shall not dream of any *other* world, whether before my life, or above me, or after my life. Wonderfully, by giving up metaphysical ideas of substance and identity, I find myself able to coincide exactly with the flow of my own be-ing in time. I can at last give up all anxiety about the future, and say a simple Yes to my life, *now*. **All this is all there is,** and **this is It**. Strangely, what Buddhists call *anatta*, the no-self doctrine, turns out to be very joyful.

Thus the modern idea of life, which since about the time of Hegel has very slowly become common property and is now firmly embedded in our everyday language, can do for us something of what religion is expected to do: it can fully reconcile us to the human situation, and can make us indestructibly – or 'eternally' – happy.

Notice too that on the account given here we do not attempt to reconcile 'science' and 'religion'. Instead, we simply point out that they are different activities, that build their different worlds in different ways. Science joins up its world by positing mathematical regularities running right across it. The Book of Nature, as seventeenth-century writers put it, is written in the language of number. A world full of built-in regularities, modelled mathematically, is a world which is in many ways predictable, intelligible and controllable. By contrast, the Book of Life is written in our natural human language of words. Our poets, artists and religious thinkers join it up and make it morally intelligible and emotionally habitable by finding metaphors and symbolic relationships running right across it. The greatest and most powerful of these metaphors have to do with life, water, light and fire; with the Sun, the Fountain, and be-ing. They have great power to make our world 'meaningful', evocative, and richly beautiful. They *embed* us in our world.

Notice here that whereas science insists upon keeping its vocabulary as precise, univocal and strictly defined as possible, religious and poetic thinking positively *relish* the biggest and loosest words, with the widest range of uses and meanings. Science is precisionist and disciplined in its use of language, insisting on getting things definite and measurable; whereas religious thought is poetical, evocative and reconciling. It aims to make me feel able to say Amen to my own life. 'See Naples, and die'? – Love life, and die. Pass on, pass away.

A good example of the point being made here is given by the best poetry of Dylan Thomas (1914–53). His vocabulary is of course very rich indeed. For 'life' he will often prefer to use a word like 'green', and for 'time' he may prefer the word 'age'. Here he is, on the subject of this present discussion. He is talking in an almost Wordsworthian way about the happiness of his childhood, in 'Fern Hill':

Oh as I was young and easy in the mercy of his [time's] means
Time held me green and dying
Though I sang in my chains like the sea.

And in the 'Poem on his [35th] Birthday':

> . . . the closer I move
> To death, one man through his sundered hulks,
> The louder the sun blooms
> And the tusked, ramshackling sea exults . . .

An important, but quite difficult corollary of this discussion is that in both religion and philosophy we should avoid the *scientism* that seeks a single, closely defined final vocabulary that will make it easier to draw a clear dividing line between the faithful and heretics. Leibniz, and a number of other scientizing philosophers since, have been much too keen on the idea of objective, apodictic Truth. It is a fantasy, and we have every reason to suspect the motives of those who pursue it and claim to possess it. They would probably like to enthrone one true system of the world, and one great Regime of objective Truth.

Well, there isn't any such pre-established reality. Apart from us, apart from the motion of our language and other sign systems, there is only Chaos, white noise, the jostling dance of the possible struggling to get out into actual expression. There is no single ready-made cosmos, no single true account of the world, and no vocabulary that cuts up the world the way the world cuts itself up. Because the world is interpretatively very plastic and plural, and wobbles forever back and forth over the brink of nothingness, religion and philosophy never come finally to rest. They never reach their goal. Like art, they go on and on, making and remaking our world. Hence the slogan, **Make, believe.**

4

Living in the Last World

By now, surely, most of the historic functions of religion have been taken over by other agencies: science, art, social work, psychotherapy and so on. Is there any abiding need left that only religion can supply?

I suggest that religion may still provide *a moral cosmology*. Science makes its observer so detached and abstract that it effectively leaves him out and so creates what it really wants, namely a diagrammatic and morally neutral picture of the world and of our place in it that helps us to envisage and to create powerful technologies. But philosophy and religion point out that we are ourselves embedded in our world, and we are valuing beings, with an interest in life, and with a need to plan our own lives. For us, our world cannot be value-neutral. We need a picture of the world as a theatre for our moral action, as our *scene*. Secular religious thought may then help us to see the human life-world as the scene of our religious feeling and our moral action; and while it is thus giving us a moral world-picture, religion can also help us to accept life, with its contingency, its finitude and its ups and downs, as a package deal. Such an acceptance of life helps us to cope with it all.

At this point I need to introduce a vocabulary given to us by Leibniz, in his *Theodicée* of 1710. He distinguished three kinds of evil – moral, natural, and metaphysical, and I suggest that it is the *third* of these that matters today.

1 MORAL EVIL, human sinfulness, was a main concern of religion until the seventeenth century. It was felt to be of cosmic significance, and needed a cosmic remedy. Today, however, we

surely feel that better parenting, education, and political arrangements can gradually make us kinder.

2 PHYSICAL EVIL – suffering, pain – became a main concern of religious thought from roughly 1680 to 1960, the period during which God was dying. Why has the world-Designer apparently designed into his law-governed world so much suffering? But today we no longer look for a *religious* explanation of and remedy for suffering. Technology, and especially modern medicine, have put it within our grasp to give almost everyone a full span of reasonably good and culturally rich life. We can do a great deal to combat and correct Nature.

3 METAPHYSICAL EVIL, or finitude – that is time, chance, and death – is today's principal remaining religious problem. In the past, religion prepared us for life in another world beyond this one. Today, though, people increasingly recognize that there is no life after death, and that we are *already in* the last world we'll ever know. We are hurtling forwards into simple extinction; passing away all the time. How can we say a happy Yes to life, when it's slipping away from us so fast, and so inexorably? How can we believe in any unchanging truths or values, when *everything* is so transient?

In short, we need a religion for people who live their brief lives in one world only, *this* world; a religion that will enable us to find eternal value in the midst of pure transience; a religion that will help us to say a great Yes to our life as we are living it out. Not a religion of deferred salvation and post-dated cheques, but a religion that delivers something that deserves to be called 'eternal happiness' and delivers it *now*.

What we have inherited from the past is something entirely different, namely a religion that requires us to believe upon authority an elaborate system of doctrines about a great invisible supernatural world and our relations with it; a religion that requires us to keep our attention fixed upon the supernatural order and promises us that if we conform loyally and do all the right things it will secure for us eternal blessedness, not now but later, in the heavenly world after we die. This life is wretched, but stick to Mother Church and she'll see you through to a better place hereafter.

Notice that in this second religion, which I call 'Church-Christianity' or 'Catholicism', we live two lives at once, like a secret agent. We live an ordinary and outwardly respectable life alongside other people in the present world, 'having your conversation honest among the Gentiles' as the Apostle puts it (1 Peter 2.12, AV); while at the same time we are living like spies, constantly in secret communication with another Government in another, and future, world. As another early Christian writer puts it 'Our true and permanent allegiance is not to the present political order, because we look to and live by a polity that is yet to come' (Hebrews 13.14).

In the New Testament we find a strange mixture of these two very different religions. What happened, it seems, was that the original Jesus preached the first of them, which I usually call 'Kingdom religion', or 'solar living'. It is a secular religion of active self-outing. A human being is not a substance, an immortal soul, but only a one-way process. I *am* my own life. One burns and burns out with love for life and for the fellow human. Living all-out, *solar* living, is what some New Testament writers think of as eternal life, now and in the present moment. When you live like that you are not on the way to any other world. You are already in the last world, and you have left mediated religion behind. There is no objective God and no supernatural order. We have abandoned the metaphysics of substance. Instead, we become completely self-identified with our own outpouring transience, and that is it. We live by self-outing and self-giving: we live a dying life, burning like a candle until we burn out. To live *all-out*, completely identified with and even *affirming* one's own transience is to live in an eternal Now, as God was said to do. In effect, God has become fully internalized as a kind of inner fire.

The original Jesus preached this religion. So far as he could be understood at all by those who made their livelihood out of a form of two-worlds, mediated religion, he had to be regarded as a heretic and a blasphemer, and – quite rightly, from that point of view – he was executed as a troublemaker. Then over the next fifty years his legacy, the first kind of religion, was gradually converted into the second, and he became the basis for a re-launch of everything that he had promised to free people from. He had been a *disobedient* Son of God: his religion involved the end of objective theism. God was fully internalized, and was no longer seen as an external lawgiver. There was no longer any supernatural world: religion was simply lived out, rather than believed. As it turned out, however, after Jesus' death his own immediacy was gradually lost, as he was turned into an *obedient* Son of God, who says to the last, 'Not my will, but Thine, be done' (Luke 22.42), and looks to God for his own long-term vindication in the world to come.

Nietzsche is the one thinker who grasps, or half-grasps, what has been happening here. As he says: 'There has been only one Christian, and he died upon the Cross.' The religion Jesus preached came to an end with him. In the Galilean teaching we were given a brief glimpse of an entirely new human world, the *last* world. Then the Oedipal revolt was crushed, and the Law of the Father was reinstated. Church-Christianity developed in order to keep Jesus dead and buried. It tried to cover up all traces of the original message by reinterpreting it away; but fortunately it was not altogether successful. Enough survived to allow for the telling of this present story.

The original Jesus, I am suggesting, was almost certainly a moral teacher who stood at the long-awaited 'end of the world' and urged his hearers to start living the last kind of life now. There is excellent historical evidence that he was regarded by many as a heretic and a blasphemer who was at least lax about, and often opposed to the entire apparatus of religious Law and mediated religion. Instead he taught a markedly *celebratory* lifestyle. One should live expressively, from the heart, without any *ressentiment* or negative feeling. One should be transparent, completely explicit, purely outgoing, and burning with love for life in general and for the neighbour in particular. One should live purely generously, in the present. Jesus did not teach any sort of inwardness or mystical discipline. He did not see the religious life as involving special dealings, via rituals etc., with a supernatural order. He seems to have been an 'ecstatic naturalist', and a pioneer of our humanitarianism.

Because he taught the end of the received heaven-and-earth, two-worlds dualism; because in effect he announced the end of religion as it had been known hitherto, he was rightly seen as a heretic, and was executed. Nobody yet thought of him as the Messiah, or as being risen from the dead. But small circles of followers, in Galilee and in Jerusalem, tried to preserve the memory of his teaching. It is to be noted here that the first 'Gospels' were not the elaborately mythicized narratives about Jesus' life that we know today: they were no more than small collections of his remembered sayings. There was as yet no interest in theologizing Jesus' person and the story of his life: only the sayings counted.

Then in the late 40s there began a sharp power-struggle for leadership of the little community. James, the Lord's brother, and one or two others of Jesus' family were dominant in Jerusalem, while Peter and others of Jesus' surviving earliest associates still lived in Galilee where they had been born. In Galilee there was a tradition that Mary of Magdala – a fishing village ten miles from Capernaum, where Jesus himself had a house (Mark 2.1, in the Greek, and note the variant reading) – had experienced hallucinations of Jesus after his death. To this day such hallucinations of someone recently dead whom one has long known very well are common. Building on this tradition, Peter developed the idea that Jesus was not simply dead, but had been exalted to the heavenly world as Messiah designate. Soon he would return in glory to establish the new world order that he had preached.

The new theology caught on fast, and was accompanied by vivid religious experiences. The risen and gloried Jesus was soon seen not only by Peter but also by the rest of the Galilean disciples. Soon, they also developed stories about the Resurrection and the Empty Tomb. So they *had* to shift at least part of the action to Jerusalem. But now read Matthew 28 and Mark 14 closely: Mary, and then Peter, discover the Empty Tomb in Jerusalem, but the narrative immediately insists that the action is transferred to Galilee, where the important commissioning visions occur. Then, subsequently, Jesus is seen by James, by the Jerusalem 'apostles' generally, and finally by an able newcomer from the Hellenistic synagogues named Paul of Tarsus (1 Corinthians 15.3–8).

Thus a quite new religion first came into being. It was 'catholic' or universal, because it included both Palestinian Jews led by James, and Hellenistic Jews with even perhaps a few Gentiles, led by Paul; and it was apostolic because it came to be ruled by an 'apostolic' priestly caste headed by Peter, who claimed to derive their authority directly from the risen Lord. The religious society was a brotherhood of pilgrims, or an army on the march, led by an all-powerful – and of course male-only – officer class who controlled doctrine, creeds and sacraments, and religious Law. Above all, it was a society of amphibians – people who still lived in the old world but did so in the power of their convictions about the invisible, exalted Jesus and the coming of his new world. They were disciplined, vigilant, expectant. They hoped to see the new world arrive during their own lifetimes; but if it didn't, then they hoped to see it in heaven after their deaths.

This new catholic religion developed fast. In the year 70, the fall of Jerusalem and the destruction of the Jewish Temple greatly encouraged the advent hopes of the infant Church. In the Gospels, as they developed the surviving tradition, Jesus' teaching was extensively revised and supplemented to reflect the new religious outlook, and the story about his life was elaborated to reflect the new doctrines about him. And remember that the Easter faith, in Jesus' exaltation to the heavenly world and his appointment as messiah designate, only began some 15 years or so after his death. It took far longer than 'three days', because there was so much to be worked out.

The surviving traditions of Jesus' teaching were already rather various, and the principal evangelists, the three synoptic gospel writers, revised in somewhat different ways the materials they received. But in Chapters 5 to 7 of Matthew's Gospel, in the so-called 'Sermon on the Mount', we have a particularly vivid example of the survival in our present text of both the religions that I have described – *both* of them being presented as taught by Jesus, and both lying side-by-side on the page. It is quite extraordinary that such astonishing inconsistencies were allowed to remain in his text by Matthew, and were unremarked by readers of such intelligence as Kierkegaard and Tolstoy.

Thus, in Matthew 5.13–16, the original Jesus tells his followers that they are the salt of the earth. They should make themselves conspicuous: they should shine, they should let it all hang out, they should *radiate*. They should live expressively, all out. But then in chapter 6.1–21 Jesus is presented as teaching exactly the opposite, namely a Catholic, heaven-oriented spirituality of hidden inwardness. For example, you should give donations to charity *secretly*, 'not letting your left hand know what your right hand is doing' (6.3). You should similarly pray secretly, not in public, and you should take trouble to hide the strictness of your fasting, 'so that your father who sees in secret will reward you openly'. So in Matthew 5 and 6, we are taught equally emphatically *both* to come out *and* to stay in the closet!

This brings out another difference between the two religions. The 'solar' Jesus 'takes no thought for the morrow'. He lives at the very End of the World, and in the present moment, without anxiety (Matthew 6.25–34). He's not worried about the future, because there *is* no future. But the Catholic Jesus is always 'ulterior' or long-termist: he does everything in order to store up treasure in heaven (Matthew 6.19–21). He takes the long view. The 'solar' Jesus is extremely this-worldly and short-termist; the Catholic Jesus is extremely other-worldly and long-termist. Like the later Christian Platonism, the revised Jesus draws a contrast between a perishing world below and an Eternal World above, a contrast totally unknown to the original Jesus.

The two religions are similarly opposed in their attitude to religious Law. The original Jesus did a great deal to justify the accusation that he had 'come to abolish the law and the prophets' (Matthew 5.17), but Matthew's Catholic Jesus is ultra-rigorist, and insists that he is greatly tightening up the requirement of the Law (Matthew 5.17b–37a).

One last contrast: the original Jesus notoriously recommends extreme, extravagant generosity. We should love our enemies, go the second mile, turn the other cheek, invite to dinner only people who cannot afford to ask us back, and so on. But the Catholic Jesus, on the contrary, urges prudent calculation and what one might call 'rational reciprocity'. It is all very well to love your neighbour as yourself, but 'Pure Love' – love even for one's *enemy* – is irrational. Interestingly, the Council of Trent (1545–63) plainly condemned the teaching of the solar Jesus, and endorsed the teaching of the Catholic, Aristotelian Jesus.

Enough: we could continue for some time yet drawing these contrasts, but the argument has some way to go. How can we be really sure which of these two religions came first? The religion that I have called 'catholic' must represent a secondary adaptation of the original teaching to the situation of Jesus' followers 20 years after his death. Jesus himself had been a kingdom man, a one-world person, an emotivist for whom everything, including one's own self, is continually pouring out and passing away. For him, only the here and now exists. We don't just live in time, we *are* time. One *is* one's own outpouring life, and one should live expressively, all-out and in a kind of standing Now, like God, or like the sun, or like a fire. One should be transparently given over to others. One should live the completely explicit and self-giving life of the Kingdom, the last life in the last world. And that, *that* is the true union of time and eternity in the Now moment. By contrast, the teaching I've called catholic is an adaptation of the tradition to the new situation of someone for whom Jesus himself is now an unseen object of devotion, securely enthroned in the heavenly World Above. The believer finds himself still living in the lower world and looking up vigilantly, hopefully. He's an amphibian: 'Come, Lord!', *maranatha*, he cries.

So the beginning of faith in the risen and exalted Jesus was also the end of the supremely great new and final religion that Jesus had preached for a year or two in Galilee, and the New Testament is a sad record of disappointment and loss. Church Christianity made Jesus into an obedient self-abnegating Son of God, and rewarded him by making him into a Cosmocrator, Christ Almighty; but it was all far less than what Jesus had glimpsed and briefly revealed, in the most sublime teaching yet heard on earth.

Our conclusion interestingly reverses the message of Albert Schweitzer. Schweitzer said that 'the quest of the historical Jesus' had been undertaken in the hope that when discovered he might become the basis for a reform and renewal of Christianity. But the quest had discovered a deluded prophet of the End of the World, dominated by a luridly supernatural philosophy of history – a figure who was quite irrelevant to us.

I disagree. After the end of Platonism and the metaphysics of substance, we have quite recently come to see ourselves as humans living in the human life-world, beings who are utterly transient in a world that is utterly transient. The Death of God entails also the Death of the World and of 'the Soul'. The last of the old optimistic Grand Narratives about the future of humankind broke down a generation or more ago. Economically and environmentally, the human future now looks very dark. It offers no bright prospect either to the individual or to the species as a whole. We probably don't *have* any long-term future. Suddenly, we feel very close to the end of our world, and it is time to dig out, and to try out, the message of the original Jesus that the New Testament attempted to bury. Solar living is the best we have, or could have. It's all we've got, now.

Appendix

In a copy of the RSV, turn up Matthew 5 and 6. With a high-lighter, mark up 5.13–16, 5.38–47, and 6.25–34. These passages together give a vivid impression of the teaching of the original Jesus.

Then with a different coloured highlighter, mark up 5.17–35, 5.48, 6.1–21 and 6.24. These passages give an impression of the 'catholicized' Jesus.

A number of passages have been left unallocated, for various reasons. They are 5.1–12, 5.36f., 5.48 and 6.22f., and they call for more detailed analysis. But almost everything ascribed to Jesus in early Christian writings reflects one stage or another in the complex transformation of the original Jesus into the ecclesiastical, or Catholic, Jesus.

Elsewhere, I have suggested that if we are ever to disentangle this process fully, we should start with the strange relationship between the two Morning Stars, Jesus and Lucifer. A neat give-away to get thought going is Bishop Heber's hymn: 'Brightest and best of the Sons of the morning . . . Guide where our infant Redeemer is laid.' The good Bishop confuses Lucifer with the Star of Bethlehem, and, better still, also with the Devil who will lead him to Jesus. Why? And why do people still not notice the oddity even today? Is the anomaly already implicit in Matthew 2.1–12?

5

Forgetting the Self

Late classical antiquity in the Eastern Mediterranean world was an age of anxiety. In Hellenistic sculpture and in the painted portraits of the dead produced in the last period of pre-Christian Egypt we encounter in almost every face an intense and troubled subjectivity. People were extremely worried about death, about their sins, and above all about their chances of personal salvation.

Hegel called the dominant outlook of this period 'spiritual individualism'. It was an age in which your single most important concern in life was to secure the eternal salvation of your own soul. To this end, the individual might feel required to flee from his public and social responsibilities and seek holiness in the desert – a flight which of course also involved rejecting even the basic biological and family imperative to beget and to raise the next generation, and instead vowing to remain a celibate. That is hatred of life. Early Christianity, marketing itself to an age that already thought in such terms, soon became extremely pessimistic and otherworldly in its outlook. Church buildings, for example, became richly decorated with mosaics, icons, stained glass and frescos; but everything that was to be seen within the building belonged to the world of the dead, the supernatural world. Indeed, the building was like a cinema foyer; it was the foyer of Heaven. Pictures on the walls lured you to go further in. Not until well into the second millennium was there anything that could recall your attention to this earth.

Being celibate, the serious first-millennium Christian battled against temptation and struggled for self-mastery. In short, he developed an intense interest in his own psychology. Besieged by evil spirits, he was comforted by the example and the gracious assistance of various good spirits, both finite and infinite. Thus, if the chief concern of the early Christian was with personal salvation, this concern manifested itself in his daily dealings with the various spirit-beings who were fighting for his soul. His chief interest in life was the state of his relations with various quasi-personal spirits – a subject traditionally pictured in Western art as 'The Temptation of St Anthony'.

From this starting point, later Western thought gradually built up the extreme personalism that remains typical of the West to this day. The Reformation doctrine of justification by faith alone sought to free the individual from domination by the external church apparatus. Just within your own subjectivity you could intuit Christ, deal with him directly, and by him be restored to God's favour. And when after Newton the new science had established a severely impersonal picture of the universe as a machine, North European Evangelical Protestantism turned to a personal experience of salvation gained by personal faith in Jesus as saviour.

The Romantic movement was yet more interested in psychology. It set out to cultivate and explore the highest attainable levels of subjective consciousness, and – originally, and very strikingly – idealized the brother-sister relationship. It begins to be clear that the main reason why many people desire life after death is no longer that they yearn for union with God, but that they desire to be reunited with their lost *human* loves. A new argument for life after death begins to be heard: Every human individual is unique and uniquely valuable, so that if we are assured that there is an all-powerful and good God, who will let nothing that is truly good be forever lost, we may trust him to restore to us those whom we have loved.

Personalism goes still further in the Western cult of the artistic and intellectual genius. It could never have occurred to the princely Esterhazys that a lowly employee of theirs such as Joseph Haydn might one day be thought more important than any of them. But from Beethoven onwards adulation of the creative genius becomes strong: authentic texts are established, canons of great national thinkers and artists are defined, and it becomes very important to be able immediately to identify whom you are listening to – whether it be Haydn, Mozart, Beethoven, or Schubert. Why? I do suspect that to this day most of us listen to great music with the idea that we are communing with the spirit of the composer. Every authentic work has its creator's unique personal stamp upon it – and *that* is what the connoisseur learns to discriminate quickly and accurately, because it is what gives to the work its value. Nothing is more enjoyable and beneficial to us than communing with a master spirit, via one of his 'signature works'.

All this implies a very intense personalism, such as is not to be found in the traditions of Indian or Chinese music, or painting, or sculpture. A corollary of it is the unique prominence of biography and of the memoir in Western literature. Interesting figures from the past – struggling women writers such as the Brontës, and male writers who had problems with their women, such as Thomas Hardy and Ted Hughes – can be sure of at least one new biography every twenty years or so, even in cases where no fresh primary material is forthcoming.

So much do people regard the unique individual self as foundational, that they often seem to think that by studying the writer's personality you can save yourself the labour of contacting him or her less directly by studying his or her *œuvre*. This is true even of some figures whose *oeuvre* is quite brief and straightforward. Thus the number of people keen to read Ray Monk's large biography of Wittgenstein is far greater than the number who can be persuaded to peruse the first 50 or 60 pages of the great man's *Philosophical Investigations* (1953). And this, despite the fact that Wittgenstein's own writing is very clear and good in that particular passage. It seems that most people think that if they know the man through a biography, there will not be much more to be learnt from his work.

It appears, indeed, that we do very often regard the work and the character of the artist as being on the same level – so much so, that if one be impugned, the other is also seriously threatened. Is it right that, if Eric Gill was as priapic and as much a child sex abuser as we are now assured he was, his work should continue to be so prominently displayed in many great churches? And what about the Nazi sympathies of Heidegger, the misogyny of Degas, the morals of Caravaggio, the racism of Aristotle . . .? The West's personalism can run close to mere prurient curiosity, a curiosity that often ends by compromising the reputation of the artist or 'thinker', and the esteem in which his work is held.

Other cultures are remarkably different. A Westerner in a great church is surrounded by memorials to, and indeed the *remains* of, the dead. But the mosque is bare, and the strictest Muslims prefer to lie in unmarked graves. Apart from such obvious cases as the woodblock printers of Japan, the names of Buddhist artists and sculptors are hardly preserved at all. The most extreme case is that of Nagarjuna, an important thinker of whom we know nothing – not even his approximate dates and country of residence.

Buddhist texts are most insistent on the value of completely forgetting the self. The Buddha has his own beloved disciple, Ananda; but in general special friendships and personal relationships do not have in Buddhism the kind of importance they have always had in Christianity. Nevertheless, Buddhist saints have a much better reputation than Christian saints and monks for being relaxed and happy. There are many laughing Buddhas, but there has been no laughing Christ in all of Christian art, nor even a Jesus engaged in animated dispute. Jesus is too weighed down by the burden of his own destiny to have any time for laughter. In company his mouth is closed, and he seems a little distant.

A curious contrast: in Christianity from the earliest times, your chief concern was for the salvation of your own soul. Above all, you must not 'sell' your soul. You needed to be ultra-long-termist and never light-headed. By contrast, the Buddhist monk *has* no soul, and is resolved not to accept salvation until he has seen all other humans, and all other sentient beings, go through the gateway to Enlightenment before him. The ordinary Mahayana monk, who *has* no self, seems habitually to be more ecstatically selfless than any Christian. Buddhist writers make the point repeatedly: the path is walked, but no one walks it; the pages turn, but nobody turns them; the book is read, but nobody reads it. . .

After a lifetime of Christian personalism, I have recently learnt the same lesson myself. I have written elsewhere of the comfort there is in the sight of one's grandchildren, as if I have thought that in them a little bit of me will survive. But more recently I have been noticing myself looking with admiration at *every* small child to be seen in the street. I'm on the way out, but it doesn't matter. While this one and that are well cared-for and happy the human race has a future, and my non-existence will not matter a damn. The beauty and the evident promise of a child can free one from self-conscious anxiety about death, and make one feel perfectly ready to step down and make way for them.

The contrast is now clear, and remarkable. The extreme Christian personalist is nowadays best exemplified by an Evangelical protestant. He says that the most important thing in life is to gain peace with God and the assurance of final salvation. The only way to gain *that* is through an intense person-to-person committed relationship with Christ, which is conducted within the sphere of one's own subjectivity. The core assumption is that everything, *everything*, that is most important in life – religion, philosophy, ethics, etc. – is mediated by subjectivity, by *personal* inwardness. All other concerns – science, engineering, economics – are merely technical and 'external'. They do not *touch* us deeply, and cannot do so. And the self? – it is a theatre of war in which everything, everything, is decided.

A quite independent illustration of the same core assumption at work is the case of Wittgenstein, already mentioned. By common consent, Wittgenstein was a very remarkable man, and perhaps a 'genius'. Knowing him well would do us a lot of good. Ray Monk's biography gives perhaps the best and most vivid impression so far of Wittgenstein the man. Having read it, we have what we were looking for, and there is no need to acquaint ourselves with his philosophy. If you can commune with the personality of the artist, you hardly need bother with the artworks; and the new Evangelical convert who has a personal knowledge of his Saviour knows everything that matters, and has no need at all to study theology. He has become an instant expert on everything – or so he appears to think.

At the opposite extreme to all this, an alliance of Buddhist and Western philosophers will assert that extreme personalism has no effective defences against fantasy, self-deception and psychological 'inflation'. The best way to happiness in religion, and the best way to knowledge by critical thinking, both require us to distance ourselves inwardly from all our own idiosyncrasies. We don't know ourselves, and we do not have mastery over ourselves, anywhere near as much as we like to think. Great figure though he was, Descartes overrated our self-knowledge. We need to set aside everything about ourselves that is *merely* personal: that is, we should forget the self. Where knowledge is concerned, we should stick to publicly tested and approved methods, and we should give our whole attention to the matter or the task that is presently before us. Selfless attentiveness is a much better Way than *Sturm und Drang*.

There is an affinity here between Buddhist teaching, some kinds of Catholic meditation, and critical thinking. All of them will advise us to 'suspend belief', to distance ourselves inwardly from all our own personal idiosyncrasies, and to wait or 'wait upon' what is before us in a completely calm, empty and attentive way. Don't *wrestle* with It; whatever It is, give it time to show itself.

William Wordsworth and Søren Kierkegaard were widely different characters, but they shared the high Romantic view that everything is mediated by us by our own subjectivity. For them, the proper study of mankind is . . . the self, its *Bildung*, its growth and its powers, its sickness and its health, and its ways of relating itself to truth. But today it seems that we have at last come to the end of that way of thinking. Instead, it seems that the way of forgetting the self is a better way to truth, with a greater range of spiritual possibilities, and with the bonus that it liberates us from the fear of death. A high degree of self-consciousness is too closely associated with *ressentiment*: it is too liable to brood, to fester, to become self-poisoning. Self-forgetfulness, by contrast, is solar: the self pours itself out, empties itself, goes out into expression all the time. It *lives* by dying, and it has no fear.

6

Impressionism and Expressionism

Now that it is fading we begin to see clearly how odd the old Western culture was. Its binary structures of thought come into view as they gradually slip away from us, and we find ourselves wondering how we were able, not long ago, to take utterly for granted such surprising combinations of ideas.

For example, the contrast I've been drawing between the penultimate world – that is, the last world but one, in which religion is mediated by priestly and scriptural authority, by religious Law and supernatural doctrine – and the true last world, was an effect of the body/soul distinction. The material, physical human body is part of this present world, the natural world, the visible creation. The body is corruptible, mortal, and even 'made of blood'. Its sufferings are 'the passions': it wears out and it dies. The body is 'common' or profane, but it is sanctifiable by Grace, having been designed to be animated by a rational soul, which by its nature properly belongs to the sacred supernatural world, the invisible world above. So we gather that the period of our life here below has been designed to serve as a period of probation, proving and testing, in preparation for the blessedness of the soul's future life in the blessed World Above. The body was a drag, a handicap, both a weight and a source of temptations. Carrying it around for a 70-years' training period helped to toughen up the soul.

In Christian art, we sometimes see an angel carrying off a dead man's soul. It is small and precious: the angel carries it delicately in a napkin; and it does indeed look almost like a naked child. It is innocent, pure and vulnerable. It is *impressionable*, as one might say, for we now understand that our chief task among all the various temptations and distractions of this life is to keep our souls as pure, virginal and unsullied as possible. Do you recall the great Liberal politician, W. E. Gladstone deciding that women are 'too pure' to have the vote? Being especially vulnerable and liable to permanent defilement, women need for their own good to be kept in protective seclusion, while their menfolk bear the burden and heat of the day for them. That is what most religious men have thought, and in many cases still think, over most of the human world.

Against this background we understand why the truly religious person had a basically *defensive* attitude to life. Any mingling, any involvement in exchanges with the world and with other people is risky because it may besmirch the soul. The holiest person is a monk, from *monos*, alone and *monachos*, 'solitary' – a person who lives alone. Today one may easily forget that the coenobitic life of monks in monasteries, and of contemplative nuns in convents, was not at first intended to be a *communal* life. No: it was more like the regulated life of a cluster of solitaries. In Eastern Orthodoxy monks have always been idio-rhythmic (each sets his own rule), and in the West the strictest contemplatives still live in architecturally contrived solitude. In a great Charterhouse each monk lives segregated and silent in a maisonette of his own.

The safest form of the good life is the solitary life. But some men must live and work in the world, and children must be born and raised in the world. There has to be secular or worldly life, and fortunately the sacrament of penance and the other means of Grace are provided, to give us all the best chance of 'dying in a state of grace'.

Against this background you can see why I am talking about the 'impressionism' which does not picture us as ever being *actively* engaged with life, but rather as vulnerable to being *marked* by life. Like the great René Descartes in France, the British empiricists continued to work with various deep assumptions that went back through the Middle Ages and early Christianity, to Plato and even earlier. As we pass through this life of ours, the world prints or impresses images of itself, 'sense impressions', upon our retinas, eardrums and other sensory surfaces, and they prompt feeling responses within us. Our emotions are understood in sadly *passive* terms: they are 'the passions', not active but reactive or responsive. Similarly, the eye is like a camera upon which the external world prints pictures of itself. Old pictures are stored in our memories, and as for thinking – that's just image processing, as we now call it. And note that the whole empiricist story about the life of the mind pictures us as the spectators of our own unfolding lives. Everything is presented to us and printed upon us. Take a word like 'character'. It is the Greek word for a stamping tool, such as a seal, a fount of type, or a Chinese wooden 'chop'. The tool makes a distinctive mark upon the smooth virgin surface of a clay or wax tablet, or skin, or a sheet of paper. Hence the idea that my whole character as a person is the sum total of all the impressions printed upon me by my experience of life. All the movement is from outside to inside, inwards, towards me. No wonder that I need to be vigilant, and to be wary of what the changes and chances of this mortal life may do to me. And no wonder that Jesus recoils gracefully from the (possibly amorous) advances of Mary of Magdala in Titian's painting (National Gallery; and see John 20.17). The holier you are, in the old scheme of thought, the more you shrink from bodily contact. Which no doubt is why Jesus in so much of Western art is embarrassingly often silent, withdrawn, passive and rather pained-looking. He doesn't care to be touched.

A strange irony: as Ernest Renan said, 'It was love that raised Jesus.' Mary of Magdala had grown up only a few miles from Jesus. She quite possibly had known him well for a long time, well enough to experience real-seeming hallucinations of him after his premature death, just as so many of the bereaved do to this day. In which case, the birth of the Easter faith in Jesus' resurrection was perhaps triggered off by just the all-too-human kind of love that fully developed Christianity so much deplored. I like that – and of course painters and authors have hinted at it for many centuries.

The view of our life that I have called 'impressionist', then, sees the events of life as marking us, often indelibly. You don't create your life: it is something that is given to you, that happens to you, and is a destiny that you must accept. The whole story is very realistic, even to the point of being deterministic. Everything is out there, prior to us, and coming down into us. We may watch our lives unfold, but we were not really thought of as the *creators* of our own lives until quite recently. Before then, we were pawns, we were the spoils of war for which God and Satan contended against each other. Belief in God was normal, and standard orthodox theism is and always was heavily predestinarian. Remember that if you try to rebel against the Will of God, you will still be fulfilling it. The almighty Creator has pre-seen and preordained everything that we say or do, including both our attempted revolt against him and our punishment for it. For good or ill, we must act out the script that has been written for us. Nobody can escape from his appointed role in the cosmic battle between good and evil powers.

The movement in the old scheme of thought was always from outside inwards. Everything came to us from God – all value, all objectivity, all order, meaning, and truth. We did not create knowledge for ourselves; God gave us knowledge, by special revelation, by inspiration, and by divine illumination of the mind, often *via* canonical writings. Western teachers who encounter Muslim education are often surprised by the extent to which Muslims still maintain that classical Arabic and the study of the Qu'ran together comprise a complete education. If there are other subjects in the curriculum at all, there will still be a strong desire to show that the Qu'ran presides over the whole world of knowledge, and that all knowledge is in a broad sense derived from it. Westerners tend to forget that not long ago they thought much the same about the Bible.

Impressionism is then 'theological', at least in its historically deepest assumptions. It is very keen on *branding*. Everything came down from above, as it was scripted to do, and impressed itself upon us. Only during the eighteenth century did a great Reversal, and a change to Expressionism, begin to take place. The shift turns out to be so big and difficult that it is not fully completed, even yet.

Our brief summary of the change might go as follows: the old culture was Tradition-directed and based chiefly upon the authority of *mediated* religion: its Law, its scriptures, its high priests and so forth. This kind of religion tends to develop theologies on a large scale. The world was constructed downwards from God, and because God was objective, infinite Being itself, all-knowing and all-powerful, his created world was objectively and permanently *the* world. His knowledge of it was perspective-less and absolute. And we could *share* in this certainty. Right up to (and even beyond) the Protestant Reformation, religious truth was metaphysically certain, and of course immutable. Against such a background error had no rights (to quote a Catholic maxim), and the dissenting individual had no chance at all.

Within Islam, an equally grand and (as it may seem) equally impregnable scheme of thought still survives. Why then did it break down within Western Christendom? From the thirteenth century prosperity grew, the lay sphere of life – both domestic and political – gradually began to assert itself, and travel and trade were making people aware of alternatives to their own local set-up. From the fourteenth century, Wycliffe, Huss and others among the inferior clergy began to question the historical evidence and the arguments that Church authority had customarily used to defend Tradition. And then, perhaps most important of all, between Copernicus (1543) and Newton (1687), the Church lost control of cosmology, and a new human way to knowledge triumphed. For a long time it was not easy to spell out adequately exactly what the new method was, and why it was so powerful. You could put the main emphasis upon the appeal to experience and experiment; upon the development and application of new mathematical tools; upon the intellectual creativity involved in finding the right questions to ask, and in developing mathematical models to explain the observed phenomena; or upon the process of 'peer review' by which new ideas were checked out within the leading learned societies. But whatever detailed account be given of these matters, it was very soon evident to all that the Moderns had eclipsed the Ancients. For the moment, nobody was quite saying: 'This is the end for religious belief.' But it was clear that the new manmade kind of knowledge, generated by gifted individuals and checked out by open debate within the learned societies, corrigible and fast-changing though it might be, was an enormous advance upon the certainties of Tradition, even when protected – as they had been – by the rack and the stake. Even before Newton, the King and the Bishops had already established the Royal Society: after Newton, within a decade the public execution of heretics had come to an end in Britain.

After Newton, it might seem obvious that the philosophers would soon develop a much more activist account of the human mind as a framer and tester of hypotheses, and as a world builder. But this was not what happened – or not yet, at least. Instead, there were worries about realism. In the old theistic natural philosophy, God's absolute knowledge and power guaranteed the objectivity of this world, and of our knowledge of it. God's world was obviously *the* world. But under the new conditions we humans can no longer claim to participate in God's absolute, perspective-less knowledge of the world. The new scientific knowledge is first constructed within human subjectivity, and from evidence supplied by our human senses: for example, a scientist who sets up an experiment and takes readings must assume that his own senses are adequate and do not mislead him. But if we are always inside our own finite, human perspective and our own human senses, how can we ever get beyond our own limits, and make the jump from *our* world to *the* world?

In a word, we can't. Today the position is that our natural science is the only game in town. We are the only beings who construct any large-scale body of knowledge about a world at all, and we are always within and dependent upon our own point of view, our own senses, and our own languages. Thus the world we build around ourselves, corrigible and changing as it is, is always and only *our* world, and cannot claim to be *the* world absolutely. Science is not dogmatic metaphysics; it is just science. It is not absolute knowledge; but it is our own most disciplined and careful attempt to impose a coherent interpretation that works upon the white noise of experience. It is immensely strong, not because it is

absolute and unchangeable, but precisely because it is *a continually changing, corrigible consensus.*

On this account we are not like cameras, upon which a ready-
made world prints a picture of itself. We are active interpreters of
our own experience. Our very perception of the world is already
highly interpretative. Raw experience, prior to any interpretation,
is like white noise. It's what you see when you shut your eyes
tight, and it's what a new-born baby sees – not any thing, but only
'a blooming, buzzing confusion'. By contrast, our adult perception is culturally very highly trained, and it is from the first closely
linked with language. So raw sense experience is turned by our
minds into an orderly picture of, and story about, the world even
as we look at it. We make it make sense. We talk sense into it.
We've spent thousands of years evolving our highly refined theories about the world, and you may sometimes like to think about
the dozens of generations of ancestors who look through your
eyes, because in your ways of seeing there are still relics of theirs.
We are products of *cultural* evolution, too, as well as biological.

Now there comes an interesting complication. In the old days,
when the founding vision of the world was God's, his vision
was absolute because God was the universal creator. He saw the
world from the standpoint of eternity, as one who altogether tran-
scended space and time. But we, by contrast, are part and parcel
of the world; we are completely interwoven with it, and of course
we are ourselves studied by our own science. It follows that we
don't have a fixed nature. We are our own changing constructs.
We have evolved, culturally, all our ideas about *ourselves*: our
theories apply to ourselves, too.

What this implies can be indicated by considering a few simple
examples. One is the modern psychology of visual perception.
The neuroscientist studies the links between the visual cortex
and the language generating areas of the brain, and theorizes
about how we construct, from very meagre twitches of electricity in the optic nerve, our whole picture of the world around us.
The experimental psychologist (the person who produces habits
out of rats) studies the same topic by looking at the behaviour of
his experimental subjects. Both of them conclude that the world

is fictioned within the brain – and of course the human being whom they study cannot possibly step out of his own head and compare the world he made inside his head with the way the world looks from an independent and objective standpoint *outside* his head. The most he can claim, it appears, is that his fiction *works*.

Unfortunately, neither the neuroscientist nor the experimental psychologist is conventionally allowed to ask: 'Hey! Doesn't all this apply to *me*, too?' He or she cannot ask that, because the scientific point of view must be *assumed* to be objective and disengaged – and then no more is to be said about it.

A similar paradox arises in connection with evolutionary biology. Nietzsche noticed it at once. If Darwin is right (and he obviously *is* right), then all our sense organs, our cognitive powers, our sociability, and our entire common world picture have all been developed simply because they help us to survive and to reproduce successfully. If so, how have we come to possess the capacity for pure mathematics? Experimental studies indicate that birds may notice the difference between four eggs and three, but that leaves them still a long way short of the abilities of Georg Cantor.

A more serious problem is the following: Darwinian theory itself indicates that we ought to adopt, and we ought to stick within the limits of, a pragmatist view of truth – and in particular, of true belief, belief about matters of fact. In which case, will biologists be willing to take the same view of Darwinism *itself*? The question brings out the fact that many scientists take a strongly realistic view of the truth of their own currently established theory, and are far from pleased when historians and philosophers of science start talking blatant heresy.

This latter example brings out a point: during the eighteenth-century Enlightenment Western thought made a great effort to reconstruct all branches of knowledge around the human subject and on the basis of critical thinking and open debate within 'the Republic of Letters'. In every subject disputed questions were to be adjudicated by standards of rationality like those which have been established in courts of law. But at the same time it was more and more coming to be recognized that a human being is always an animal, a living, striving being with sense organs, desires, interests and a point of view, and above all, a being who is a product of and belongs to a particular language group, and to a cultural totality as it exists in a certain place and time.

So the world was to be rebuilt, not just around finite humanity, but around a historically, linguistically, culturally *embedded* understanding of what we humans are. Hence the changeover to 'expressionism', and to what Hegel calls *Geist*, others call just *language*, and I prefer to call *Life* or *the Fountain*.

Now you see why I've been using the terms of art: 'impressionism' and 'expressionism'. In terms of the history of painting, the changeover takes place in the 1880s, when the Impressionism of Manet, Pissarro, Sisley and some of Manet and Degas begins to give way to the Expressionism of Vincent Van Gogh, Claude Bernard, Paul Gauguin and others. All-out Expressionism is the beginning of the Modern movement: Rimbaud back in the early 70s, Strindberg, Nietzsche. Monet, 'only an eye', painted effects of light, sense impressions. Those who followed Van Gogh steadily moved away from representation and preferred instead to project out their own outpouring feeling as colour.

The philosophers whom the Expressionists (the *Blaue Reiter* group, the *Fauves*, etc.) liked most were Schopenhauer and Nietzsche. From the former they took especially the emergent idea of the human being as a driving will-to-expression. We are not pure thinking substances, grounded in a simple, perfect, eternal One. The world-ground is divided, and so are we. We are struggling to get ourselves out into expression, and so (in some measure at least) to get ourselves together and become, briefly, ourselves. Art can be seen as a great consolation, a way of becoming and affirming oneself, a way to redemption, a way of making a consoling sense of life. Nietzsche adds, very interestingly, the question: why did we go on supposing for so long that the chief End of man, our ultimate goal in life, was to attain a special, absolute, blessedness-giving kind of theoretical *knowledge*? Even in Calvinism, the child still learnt the question-and-answer: 'What is the chief End of man? To *know* God and enjoy him for ever.' But that prioritizing of theory was absurd. We humans are striving, practical beings. We are made happiest by being able fully and completely to express and fulfil ourselves in love and creative work. We want expression, and we want mutual recognition. We want to *expend* ourselves, completely. The old orientation of religion towards correct supernatural belief was a complete mistake. Salvation is solarity, living as the sun does, living from the heart, burning and burning out. That's all.

7

Lifestyle

When it first appeared in the early 1970s, the word 'lifestyle' looked like a welcome and useful addition to our vocabulary. If a 'spirituality' is a style of piety or of religious life, understood in the old supernaturalist way as a life oriented towards a distinct spirit-world or 'Heaven' beyond life, then we could mark out an important difference by preferring to use the term 'lifestyle' for a purely secular and this-worldly form of religious life. There is no higher world; all this is all there is; we are living already in the last world, and living already the last life we will ever have; our life is final, and has no outside. Do I make myself clear? There will be no retakes, no second chances, and absolutely no external valida- tion of our life, nor any reparation for the evils and misfortunes that we have suffered. We are on our last lap: but of course we cannot see beyond our last lap. We'll never see death, and we'll never know that we have ended. But although we will never verify the fact, all experience indicates that we *will* indeed die; and if we feel a desire to reach the top in life, then we will try to live our life now in the full recognition and acceptance of its finitude. Our life has no after, no beyond, no outside. We should live – especially when we get to be as old as I am – in full acknowledgement of the fact that we may very soon suddenly become extinct, cease to exist, with little or no warning. I should live each day as if it may turn out to be my last. As I go about my daily routines, I am con- scious that I have already done many things for the last time and will perhaps today do a few more things for the last time. I'm in 'the last chance saloon', as a popular phrase has it. The prospect before me is getting rapidly narrower. I need to make the most of whatever time I have left, and for that I need to love life intensely but without clinging to it. I must forget my self – a good thing to do, and in fact an easy thing to do.

Today, alas, the word lifestyle has become sadly debased. People too often use it merely to describe a particular pattern of consumption of goods and services. But I want to keep the richer sense, too. A lifestyle is a secular spirituality, and one particularly prompted by the realization that our life is finite.

The most important ethical consequence of our new (Nietzschean, and 1960s) awareness that we are already in the last world is the recognition that we must henceforth habitually think in terms not of instrumental but of intrinsic value. We are no longer in school under discipline; we are out in the adult world. We no longer do things, or accept disciplines, because they will benefit us in the long term when we graduate to the next life or the next world. What we do or value must be done or valued for its own sake and right now. We should go all-out for the paradisal world now and for solar living now, because they are not going to come hereafter. There *is* no hereafter. So they'll only come if we choose them *now*.

It follows that the Marxist/Leninist doctrine that we must accept the dictatorship of the proletariat now so that we can forge the New Man who will live in the fully communist society of the far future; and the doctrine that we must put with the Church's discipline now and live whole lives in religious vows of poverty, chastity, and obedience, so as to prepare ourselves to live, in a future world, the 'Kingdom' kind of life that Jesus preached; all doctrines that tell us to put up with hardship now, because we are being got ready for a better world hereafter, are now out of date. We are already in the last world, and there will not be any better one.

A few themes of the old, now obsolete, religion do nevertheless survive. One of them is the sense that life is urgent. Get a move on!

Eschatological urgency

Too many human lives are desperately trivial, unimportant, wasted or simply tragic. In the past, preachers and moralists might attempt to awaken people to life's finality, its *seriousness*, by warning them that 'The End is nigh'. But what End? Do you mean some great supernatural Event such as the Return of Christ in Judgement, as expected by the early Christians? Do we mean the traditional Four Last Things for each individual to consider, namely Death, Judgement, Heaven and Hell? Do we mean, more cautiously, just Death itself, 'the end of age'? Or do we mean, minimally, that life is finite and outside-less, and we should be prepared soon to find it closing, so that we should be thinking about putting our affairs in order and rounding off our life's chief concern, whatever it has been?

There is a spectrum of possibilities here. On the most thoroughgoing supernaturalist view, the preaching of the End makes it urgently necessary for us to attend to the Four Last Things, and to do all we can to prepare ourselves 'to meet our Maker', and generally to maximize our chances of gaining external happiness. On the most 'immanent' and outside-less view, we should try to give our own lives closure by sorting out our affairs so that we do not leave too many complications and burdens for our nearest and dearest. We should try to complete our work, visit our oldest friends again, and spend time 'looking our last at all things lovely', as Walter de la Mare advises in a fine poem.

The two responses to death are very different: in fact, they are literally 'worlds apart'. Accordingly, we may well consider it very important to get clear about which is the more rational. Do I seriously expect that I shall have post-mortem conscious awareness of being truly myself before God, and perhaps with others? Or do I conclude that because our life is outside-less I can never find myself outside this life of mine, and therefore can never personally verify the answer to the question about life after death? For me as an individual, life's finite, and I'd better make the most of it while I can and make such provision for others as I can. But I'll never actually *know* I'm dead. Philip Larkin's horrors were a mistake, and the view that we do best to live by is the early Wittgensteinian view that death is not experienced or lived through. As for the old supernaturalist view that I will actually experience being myself, post-mortem, with others, outside time and before God – well, it should nowadays be disregarded. The idea that I can have a life outside my life is meaningless. The novelist Anthony Burgess, a not-quite-wholly-lapsed Catholic, continued to say, in a tone that reminds one of Pascal's Wager: 'Look, it *might* all be true'; but that likelihood is today infinitesimal. I fear it *can't* be true. In which case, the most rational opinion is as follows: (a) The Second Coming and the End of History – no; (b) The Four Last Things for the individual – no; (c) There is no post-mortem consolidation, and death is absolute exclusion and eternal loss (the Philip Larkin view) – no; and lastly (d), the Wittgenstein view, namely that our life is outsideless but finite and therefore we need to hasten to make something of it while we can – yes! The Wittgensteinian view is affirmative, adult, and free from Larkin's wretched self pity.

The correct modern view of death for today also has another advantage: it keeps a little of the old eschatological urgency: 'While we have time, let us do good unto all men . . .' (Galatians 6.10). Heidegger takes a similar 'alarm clock' view of death in his *Being and Time* (1927) under the influence of his fellow student Rudolf Bultmann, the theologian. And so should we.

Very strikingly, a number of Christian poets of the seventeenth century – the last period in which there were genuine old-fashioned believers in the orthodox Latin Christian faith – seem to agree. They sound the warning bell that tells us of 'Time's wingéd chariot, hurrying near', and point out that 'Successive nights, like rolling waves, / Carry them forward, who are bound for death' – but they mention only death, or 'the End', without actually invoking the supernatural 'Beyond' at all. George Herbert and Andrew Marvell were both of them undoubtedly orthodox ecclesiastical Christians; but they evidently think they can make their point adequately without going beyond my own purely secular view. Death is coming: therefore wake up . . . and the rest can conveniently be left unmentioned. You can fill it in in various ways, ad lib.

This ambiguity becomes very puzzling in the case of Christina Rossetti. In her oeuvre as she left it there is a group of generically

'Christian' poems in which she does affirm the Christian doctrine about what awaits us after death; but these poems are only a sub-set within the larger body of her work, in which she adopts the traditional lyric poet's pessimistic view that in death we fall into permanent sleep and oblivion, with no more than a few floating flickers of memory of our previous life: 'Haply I may remember / And haply will forget'.

When she is talking in her Christian voice, Rossetti, the disappointed unmarried woman, hopes that in death she may like a nun become the Bride of Christ and find eternal happiness. But more often she writes as a pagan lyric poet who expects to live forever underground in a state of whispering regret and loss, just like the pagan dead from Homer to Larkin. But she never comes to a firm decision about which view is actually correct, and so never decides how best to live. That's sad. Promises of post-mortem consolation led her to accept and live an inhibited churchy life under religious discipline, preparing herself for a great Cosmic Examination after death. But since our life is in fact outside-less, she ended up by frittering away the only life that she, or anyone else, will ever have. She remained stuck in uncertainty and indecision about life after death, like too many poets from Tennyson to Betjeman, 'limping with two different opinions' (1 Kings 18.21, RSV). Trying to have it both ways, she ended up with neither. Like all other modern believers in Church-Christianity, she remained stuck in half belief, permanently ironized and morally paralysed, like a theologically educated bishop who is holding on in the hope that the status quo will see him out. (They're *all* like that.) In the general culture that state of permanent ironization and moral paralysis – Western culture in acute decline – is commonly called 'postmodernism'. It is the state the churches have been in since the Rococo, and it is somewhat *camp*. Frankly, it fully deserves the mockery it attracts.

I'm another alarm clock. I'm saying, please let us decide what we really believe, and begin to act accordingly. Anything, to get ourselves out of the sick psychology of faith in severe long-term decline. We've been stuck for two and a half centuries already. That's far too long.

The last world

The original Jesus of Nazareth chose to live, and wanted us to follow him in choosing to live, in the last world, the world that has no further world beyond it, the world in which we mortals at last are strong enough to live fully affirmatively and expressively, burning and burning out. We were, for him, utterly to forget all anxiety about our own future. Because life is outside-less, and we will always simply *be* our own mortality, there really is nothing – not any thing – to fear. I am already about 90 per cent or 95 per cent burnt out now, and when I am fully expended or consumed there will no longer be any me. So I *have* – because I'll *be* – nothing to fear, and soon there will be nothing left of me to be mourned. I should have no worries.

Our cognitive fall into catastrophic religious error takes place when we start giving that word 'Nothing' a capital initial letter, and begin to be afraid of it. Remember the popular iconography of Death the Grim Reaper with his scythe, wearing a hooded black clerical cloak. It envelopes him, so that we cannot exactly see his feet, or his hands . . . or *his face*! The cloak is empty. There is nobody in it. Death is not any body. Death is an unthing that cannot be met. It is not any thing at all, just as outside life there is nothing, not even a void, because life *has* no outside. Philip Larkin, in his terrified verse, imagines that in death we find ourselves in 'outer darkness' or in the void. But there *is* no outer darkness, and there *is* no void, because life has no outside.

Now we see why and where the birth of Christianity went so badly wrong. It was desperately difficult, perhaps it seemed quite impossible, to come to terms with the horror of Jesus' death after he had in his short career attained such heights. The new message, that he was risen from the dead, that he had been exalted to Heaven, that he was now God's designated Messiah, and that he would shortly return in glory – all this, together with a good deal more that was soon to be added, seemed to be a theologically brilliant solution to the wretched situation of the infant community. Jesus and his message were not after all lost for ever. His death had shown up the extent to which the world in general, and his own people in particular, were unready for him. Their rejection of him was something of a disaster: but now there was granted a special period of Grace – the ecclesiastical period – during which the Church, organized and led by the apostles and their successors, would dispense the forgiveness of sins and give all mankind a chance to enter the Last World when Jesus returned in glory to inaugurate it for good. He would be the Terminator; he'd be back, with a vengeance. Therefore repent and join the Church!

This theological resolution of the awkward plight of Jesus' followers since his death in the early 30s seems to have been worked out largely by Peter and Paul, in Galilee and in Jerusalem, presumably during the late 40s. It is expressed in Paul's first letter to the Thessalonians. (Forget about the *Acts* of the Apostles, a work which relates only what *ought* to have happened, and doesn't tell us what *did* happen.) It is very interestingly doubled in the way the relation of John the Baptist to Jesus was constructed. The analogy goes as follows: As John preached imminent Divine Judgement and offered baptism and the remission of sins to people who would thus be made ready to hear Jesus's call to people to start living in the last world, so the first coming of Jesus similarly prepared the way for the second. For the first Jesus's call to men to start living the last kind of life now has been cruelly rejected, but now God has mercifully opened a period of Grace by creating at Pentecost the one, holy, catholic, and apostolic Church. He has given to the Church its leadership and their message, namely that Jesus is raised from the dead and exalted to God's right hand, whence he will shortly return to earth in force: 'No more water: the Fire next time!' – the Baptist's old message *redoubled*. All the more urgent then, that you should flock to the Church, and avail yourself of the forgiveness of sins and the divine grace that the Church was authorized to dispense.

All this was a very ingenious theological solution to the mess left by the tragic and horrible martyrdoms of John and Jesus. It led to vivid religious experiences, visions of the glorified Jesus, which were soon connected up with the old story that Mary of Magdala had seen apparitions of Jesus fifteen years or so earlier. The early simple conviction that Jesus was now 'Lord' soon expanded into a complex narrative. Jesus had risen from the dead in Jerusalem and had appeared, first to Mary and then to others in a carefully calculated order of ecclesiastical seniority. Then followed the commissioning of the Apostles in Galilee, the Ascension, the Heavenly Session at God's 'right hand', then Pentecost, mass baptisms, and the beginnings of regular Sunday worship on 'the Lord's day'. The new theology was thus turned into a story, a founding narrative of events which later Christians would come to believe had occurred historically – the author of Luke/Acts being one of the most influential 'enhistorizers'.

It was clever. Paul had created 'ur-catholicism' out of a few scraps, and had given the infant Church enough momentum and self-confidence to last it for some 15 centuries. But it was also terribly and disastrously retrograde. Literally retrograde – a step backwards – because the theology pushed the society of Jesus' followers back from the last world to the penultimate world, the Church being by definition a society of people who look up to a higher and greater future reality that they long to see arriving on earth. 'Thy Kingdom come.'

Note here that in popular apologetics the chain of events surrounding the post-mortem exaltation of Jesus to Heaven amount to 'the founding of Christianity'. But in fact the Resurrection of Jesus was the *Fall* of Christianity. It was a lapse back from the adult life in the last world that Jesus had preached, to life as a schoolboy in a great disciplinarian institution that trained and packaged people for life in an adult world that was now postponed into a more and more remote future. Jesus was severely falsified: instead of the freedom he had preached, believers were now to live under 'the Law of Christ'.

The final nail was driven in by the Church's eventual claim to at least some degree of jurisdiction over Purgatory, and its claim that in Heaven we would see *Ecclesia Triumphans*, the Church Triumphant. Those doctrines, together with the official ecclesiastical condemnation of 'pure love', aimed to kill off the gospel of the original Jesus forever, and very nearly succeeded.

Impossible generosity

After she had passed the age of 80, a certain grandmother allowed herself to become a little eccentric. For example, she would periodically announce that she was 'thinking of having back' some gift such as a Christmas present that she had given a few years earlier. It seems that for her there was no such thing as a gift absolute. A gift creates a relation of *indebtedness* to the donor; and how else could you properly acknowledge your continuing debt, except by being ready to return the gift to the donor on demand? The items were duly handed back.

In thinking like this, Grandmother was in distinguished company, because both God and Jacques Derrida hold (or held) similar views. There *is* something paradoxical about the notion of a pure gift – and most of all perhaps about a pure gift of forgiveness. The donor may say airily 'Think nothing of it: let's say no more about it' – but the gift is still there between the two parties, a sort of elephant in the room, an unspoken presence.

God in particular seems to be thought of as threatening to revoke what was originally a pure gift, the idea of an act of almost unthinkable generosity being one that runs right through Christianity from the first. For our original sinfulness and our actual sins we humans supposedly merit nothing but eternal damnation, but at an almost unimaginable cost to himself God has found a way of redeeming us and now offers us plenary absolution and eternal salvation. Indeed, the status of a redeemed human is actually *higher* than that of a prelapsarian human, for we were at first created to be one rung lower than the angels, whereas after our redemption we are one rung higher than even the highest angel. To put it simply, Peter Breugel's 'Hell' is what we deserve, and 'The Coronation of the Virgin' is an image of what is freely offered to us – admission to the very life of the Holy Trinity.

To this extraordinary situation, the Catholic Christian traditionally responded: '*O felix culpa!*' – O happy fault that has been deemed to merit such and so great a redemption! Similarly, the Protestant sang of 'Amazing Grace', with a slightly delirious joy.

God's Grace, thus understood, was in the strongest sense super-natural – something not possible at all in the ordinary course of things. It altogether transcends justice; it is beyond reason. Yet it turns out to be less purely unconditional than at first appeared. It demands a response from us:

> Let all bitterness and wrath and anger and clamour and slander be put away from you with all malice, and be kind to one another, tender-hearted, forgiving one another, as God in Christ forgave you.
>
> (Ephesians 4.31f., RSV)

Most scholars think these words were written by a continuator of Paul's writing and work, rather than by Paul himself. But it doesn't matter, because nobody doubts that the teaching is in his voice. By an act of absolute generosity, God has forgiven and re-deemed you; *therefore* you ought to behave in the same sort of way towards each other. The so-called 'Lord's Prayer' pictures Jesus as going a step further in his teaching: 'Forgive us our debts, As we have also forgiven our debtors', and Matthew's Jesus goes on to threaten that God's free gift of forgiveness may be revoked, for 'if you forgive men their trespasses, your heavenly Father also will forgive you; but if you do not forgive men their trespasses neither will your Father forgive you your trespasses' (Matthew 6.12, 14f.). Later in the same Gospel, Jesus is pictured as directly threatening damnation to those who have been forgiven but then have failed to forgive others (Matthew 18.23–35), which com-pletely revokes the free gift of divine forgiveness.

The conclusion I wish to demonstrate from this is that as the teaching of the original Jesus was taken up into – perhaps, 'mythi-cized into' – a great system of supernatural theology, so its real point was progressively destroyed. At the same time, the tradi-tion of Jesus' sayings was redacted, so that an ecstatic, emotivist ethic of spontaneous, 'impossible' generosity was reduced to a punitive, heteronomous ethic of religious law, backed by supernat-ural sticks and carrots. Jesus had taught the ethical insufficiency and ineffectiveness of all ordinary ideas of reciprocity, of 'getting *even*', and of 'justice' as fair shares and fair play. We'll never live the good life until we learn to live without any negative feeling, or *ressentiment*, and learn to be emotionally open, candid and completely approachable by others, *all* others. Human beings have a remarkable facility for getting into, and then becoming frozen in, chronically negative attitudes of mistrust, suspicion, distaste, hostility and so on towards each other. These negative responses become habitual and then engrained. Like bitterness, grudges, envy, and resentment, they tend to poison the soul – that is, to block the free flow of our feelings, so that they fester. Our suspicions, our prejudice, our sense of grievance and our desire for vengeance become insatiable, and slowly take over our lives. In the view of the original Jesus, we are all of us liable to get into this kind of fix. Sometimes it is because we have allowed our relationship with another individual to become soured, and sometimes it is a group problem – a question of sectarian, or ethnic, or class, or sexual, or other collective prejudice. We can and we do conjure up an amazing variety of reasons for not being able to get on with others. Anyway, Jesus' view is that in the last world we cannot permit ourselves to become locked into any form of *ressentiment*. We have to go way beyond the ethics of tit for tat, vendetta, retributive justice and 'demanding our rights'. We have to be 'big', and to behave with a degree of generosity that many ordinary people think impossible. Without that, we are nothing, and our life is worthless. We need to become as absolutely generous as life itself is. We need to *feel for* others.

In short, Jesus' main argument is secular. In the penultimate world, we may keep the rules in the hope of being rewarded (or vindicated, that word 'vindicated' being itself a specimen of *ressentiment*-fuelled thinking) in the life hereafter. But when we understand that we are *already in* the last world, then we see necessity of putting things right now, because there will be no future formal vindication, nor any better opportunity than now. Time's running out. And in order to put things right, we must ourselves take the initiative. We are all of us reluctant to risk rejection, but there are occasions when *you* must be the one who makes the first move.

A familiar example is the recent, and so far rather successful, inter-communal reconciliation in Northern Ireland. The peoples there belong to different national and religious traditions. But they have a long historical knowledge of Christianity, and many of them do recognize first, that reconciliation is a moral and practical necessity and secondly, that it demands a very costly effort to 'forgive and forget'. For years to come yet, people in public places are going to be bumping into others who a few decades ago were their bitter enemies, and perhaps even the murderers of their own kinsfolk. But somehow there must be reconciliation, costly though it is. In today's Belfast, there are still a number of walls that separate the different communities, and within these small diehard remnants there may well be people who still take pleasure in invoking the old supernatural sanctions – 'I hope he rots in hell', they say with relish. But in our hearts we all know that the best time to make the costly first move and to seek reconciliation is *now*, because reconciliation is imperative, and there will never be any better time than now to achieve it.

And all this, I insist, is a straightforward matter of *secular* morality, and a matter of human *feeling*. Mediated religion, with its system of religious Law backed by supernatural rewards and punishments, is the religion of the penultimate world, a world in which all faith and action are instrumental – that is, with a view to a Tribunal, and for the sake of something greater, that is yet to come. But Jesus announced the end of the penultimate world and the coming of the last world. He called the last world 'the Kingdom of God', because in his cultural setting that was the available term. But for him the Kingdom of God, in which mediated religion and religious Law come to an end, was beginning here on earth. It was the same as what we call 'secularism', this worldliness. It was and is the last world, with *no* further world beyond it, and in the last world value becomes intrinsic, and all moral action flows straight out of us, as an expression of our own feelings and valuations. In the last world, we all become subjective and live from the heart.

In the last world, God is no longer a cosmic lawgiver, Lord and Judge, over against us. When the prophets declared that the

The 'Kingdom' as a Secular world.

old covenant, the Law, had failed, they implied that a particular 'realistic' notion of God had failed. The remedy was the internalization of God as spirit, or as 'power', within the heart. God and the self become concentric. God coincides with and is the will to live/will to love, or libido, that wells up in us everyday. It keeps us going; we live by it. Our life and action are 'holy', insofar as we are able to be uninhibitedly generous and available to others.

Historically, Christian writers have never been able to take Jesus seriously as a thinker. In part, at least, the reason for this has been that the tradition of his teaching has been so very heavily confused and corrupted in the canonical Gospels as we have them. But another reason is theological: orthodox ecclesiastical Christians have been unable to recognize that realist theology, with its objective God, its objective supernatural world, and its objectivist ethic of religious law, natural and revealed, is merely dispensational. But the original Jesus was a prophet of the Kingdom of God, the last world, the world that has no further and greater reality beyond it. So, in our terms, Jesus was secular, because his teaching calls upon us to live in a way that closes all the oppositions – between the sacred world and the secular, between God and the self, and between duty and inclination. As a result, his ethic is of a kind that we would call secular and emotivist. He is still a whole 'dispensation' ahead of most of us.

Three amusing corollaries. In order to modernize Christianity for today, all we need to do is to reverse all the complex intellectual work that early Christians such as Paul did in the first two or three generations after his death. Paul put the clock back: we need to put it forward again.

Secondly, Luther suggests that, because in Jesus God was incarnate, the death of Jesus could be seen as the Death of God. We correct him by saying that on the contrary, the Galilean teaching of the merely human Jesus was the death of God *and* the coming of the Kingdom of God rolled into one. By the same token, the resurrection of Jesus was the disastrous *forgetting* of him and his message.

Thirdly, Jesus' solar, emotivist ethic of the heart is strongly expressivist, in a way well illustrated by Etty Hillesum's *Journal*, which begins on its first page with the young Etty examining herself. She's quite a good lover, she decides; but she does have something with which to reproach herself. When she reaches orgasm, instead of a full-throated yell, she emits mere half-strangled croaks, because she fears that someone may hear her. This she takes to be a sign that she is not being sufficiently generous. The reader smiles at Etty's scruples: a fully modern, life-affirming saint like Etty is evidently not at all like St Thérèse of Lisieux, the Little Flower. But Etty really *is* a saint: read on and see. Eventually she goes on the train to Auschwitz and death, loving and caring for her parents and the other older people and refusing to harbour any kind of *ressentiment*, to the last. For her, sanctity is solarity, wholeheartedness.

8

Our World

It took a long time to put God together. The first impulse in philosophy to seek God as the founding centre of everything goes back as far as Parmenides and Plato (both active around 500–400 BC); but it can very plausibly be argued that the *Ens Realissimum*, the Most-Real Being, the God of Western philosophical theism – the God of the three Abrahamic faiths and of Western civilization – became clear and fully developed only in the writings of Augustine (around AD 400). In the great tradition that Augustine established, the last major philosopher was Leibniz (or perhaps Berkeley, or perhaps Christian Wolff).

The great tradition of top-grade philosophical 'belief in God' lasted, then, from around AD 400–1700. In that period, God did not look like a human intellectual construct: God looked like a great public reality and philosophers, who otherwise held quite a wide range of views, were nevertheless in broad agreement about the vocabulary in which one might prove the existence of God and explain his mode of being and his attributes. Contemporary Jewish and Muslim philosophers were part of the same tradition, and held the same view of God. God was the Most Real Being, infinite and self-existent, the unifying Ground of all reality, truth and value. God held everything together and undergirded everything.

The period of greatest confidence in the public, objective reality of God was thus a sort of stretched mediaeval period that ran from the Christian Roman Empire to the West European Enlightenment. Even within that period, however, there were some remaining problems that had already been raised in antiquity, and were never to be solved. The chief one (using a now outdated vocabulary) runs as follows: God is by definition infinite, simple (that is structureless), and timeless. The human mind is the opposite: it is finite, it thinks 'discursively', and it is time-bound. How can it possibly know God? God presents the human mind with nothing that it can latch on to. Did not even Augustine himself say that 'there is no knowledge of God in the mind except the knowledge that it does not know him'? And to switch the question into a more up-to-date vocabulary: 'Given that language is what it is and works in the way it does, how can fact-stating sentences about God ever be shown to be descriptively true?'

The questions have never been satisfactorily answered, and cannot be. Indeed, it remains part of orthodox doctrine that God is incomprehensible (by a finite mind that has to think things through the categories), and ineffable (in human language, which we invented in order to transact in it the everyday business of our human life-world). So we have never been able, even at the height of the Middle Ages, to construct a truly impregnable philosophy of God.

After Berkeley and the Leibnizians, after about 1730, the major Western thinkers faced a new situation. The old God was fast fading. Did this mean that the human mind, no longer being grounded in the Divine Mind, would lose its old confidence that it could gain some knowledge of an ordered real world out there, prior to it, and independent of it? The extraordinary triumph of Sir Isaac Newton seemed to show that the human mind, just from its own resources in mathematics and sense-experience, is capable of constructing a powerful and comprehensive system of natural philosophy (or, as we would call it, mathematical physics). The job of philosophy must surely be to show how Newton had done it: to show, in short, how we humans have been able to build a powerful unified system of knowledge of a real, material world out there, independent of our minds. Can we, in short, develop on our own a system of knowledge of *our* world that we can confidently take for objective knowledge of *the* world, knowledge as sure as we formerly imagined God's knowledge of his world to be?

If the answer is Yes, then the Death of God doesn't make much difference. We can, as a French astronomer put it, get along perfectly well 'without that hypothesis'. The law-abiding material universe, the self, and knowledge still stand firm. God is, frankly, not much missed: the world gets on well enough without him.

There are today many people – especially among the more anti-philosophical scientists – who remain confident realists about scientific knowledge. They will bluffly argue that science is obviously a much better way to knowledge than theology, and it obviously delivers a better grade of knowledge. So they see no problem. If they ever wonder about how the Universe has evolved within itself a being capable of knowledge; a being in whom the Universe becomes bright, becomes conscious of itself, becomes *known*, then they may move in the direction of a conservative brand of German Idealist philosophy, or they may (and often do) stick with science, with evolutionary biology, neuroscience and psychology, and trust in the future development of these sciences to explain how it is that in us the Universe has come to know itself. That, and a dash of positivism, may be enough. They will be thoroughgoing scientific humanists, for whom the accelerating growth of our human knowledge will gradually give to man *Weltherrschaft*, world-mastery, cosmic lordship – and perhaps even the power to remake himself as an immortal.

Can such extravagantly optimistic humanism be justified? True, something very similar is common in the religions. Christ Almighty, *Christos Pantocrator* in Christian art, is a world-ruling figure who sits enthroned on the firmament or on a rainbow. Similarly, the Buddha became a cosmic figure. Hindus and Jains have ideas of the cosmos as being itself a humanoid giant. Even Islam and Judaism, with their iconoclastic traditions, have had ideas of a great Perfect Man, for whom God made the world. But all these religious ideas belong to the old mythic view of the world in which it was usual to see the self as the Microcosm and its counterpart the world as the Macrocosm. A certain symbolic harmony and correspondence between the mind and the world was built in from the first.

Modern natural science owes its huge success to the firmness with which it excluded all such ideas from the outset – ideas of hidden symbolic meanings and occult purposes. Science claimed to be mechanistic and grandly *impersonal*. Not surprisingly, immediately after Galileo people began to notice how unspeakably vast, alien and silent the modern Universe is. We'll never travel around more than the tiniest corner of it.

And what of the status of our scientific knowledge? In practice, most scientists can and do charge ahead without needing or wishing to take any notice of philosophy. But here it is worth pointing out that our natural science is a human cultural product. The world it portrays is *our* world, the world not as seen from any absolute or perspective-less standpoint but the world as seen from a human standpoint. All our scientific knowledge has been mediated through our human senses, our language, our bodiliness, our culture and history, and also by the practical interest of the ruling power that pays the bills, because it perceives some likely military, agricultural, medical or other advantage accruing. Our modern physics, for example, is one of the three or four greatest creations of the human mind, but ever since Renaissance times rulers have had an eye to its military applications. Hence all the money that has gone into it and has made it so big and beautiful. Physics is the R and D department of the military.

Science works, but it is our creation, and bears our mark upon it. Think, for example, of how politicians from the furthest Left to the furthest Right, from Kropotkin to Hitler, have sought to appropriate Darwinism. But all scientific work presupposes and refers back to the world of ordinary language and everyday life, and scientific knowledge remains just a branch of human cultural production. We know of no other angle upon the world than our own, and on philosophical grounds I suggest that Wittgenstein's aphorism is correct. He said: 'If a lion could speak, we would not be able to understand him.' *A fortiori*, there are no men in rubber reptile suits talking American out there, as science fiction writers suppose; and if we get that idiocy out of our heads, then we must admit that we have no idea of how we might be able to recognize an extra-terrestrial as being 'intelligent', or of how we might set about trying to communicate with it. All natural human languages are pretty much alike, and in principle a person who knows one can learn any other. But if we were to meet a genuine alien, how could we ever hope even to be able to recognize some of its behaviour *as* a sort-of language – and still less, learn it?

So after the Death of God, we really are radically alone in the Universe. We can't really begin to conceive of some *other* standpoint, language and knowledge-system, such as we might use to check and perhaps corroborate our own. So we've had it. We have only *our* world, and we can never get out of our human perspective upon the world. We no longer have any access to any *absolute* and perspectiveness vision of reality; and it is, I guess, very sure and nearly certain that we will never be in a position to corroborate our vision of the world by finding some other species which has scientific theory isomorphous with our own (similar particles, similar Periodic Table of the Elements, some similar laws of nature, etc.).

In short, we cannot get, and never will get beyond our own language and ways of thinking. We cannot get beyond culture in order to obtain some kind of external and independent corroboration of our ideas about reality, truth and value. Our world is outside-less, like a soap opera: it meanders on, and one never comes to any edge or any basis of it. Our world is just a theatre in which different interpretations of our existence jostle and conflict with each other forever, but no final Truth is ever reached. Indeed, we can no longer even imagine what the victory of a final Truth might be. Even the scientists find it hard to envisage science as a whole being completed, and coming to a halt.

We seem to have known about this strange modern condition since the early nineteenth century, when people first began to talk about the endless, inconclusive debate between optimists and pessimists, and about 'the climate of opinion', 'the spirit of the age', and so on.

The condition is created by a strange ambiguity. Our modern man-made knowledge, and in particular our highly developed scientific knowledge, is very large and beautiful, and it works. But because it is only human, and quite without any fully independent corroboration and grounding, it does not have and cannot gain the sense of solid reality that metaphysics and religious doctrine used to give people. Our whole man-made world that we have built to live in teeters all the time along the knife edge between being and nothingness. The old distinctions between waking and dreaming, the real and the imaginary, fact and interpretation, have become blurred, creating the condition that postmodernists call 'the disappearance of the real'. Visitors to California, or to Las Vegas, complain noisily about an environment in which reality has been entirely replaced by a pasteboard film set mock-up of itself. But that's our normal condition nowadays, after the Death of God and the end of metaphysics! We become acutely aware, more aware than ever before, of the sheer contingency of existence. Everything is fleeting, the Void yawns just a step ahead all the time. The young Kierkegaard complained that all existence terrified him – and the terror was exactly the terror you feel when you try to walk out over a clear glass floor with a huge empty space below. That's us.

But we've got to get used to it. It is our normal condition henceforth. In Japan it was called the floating world, in India *Maya*. In the West, it is best captured by the Rococo style of decoration in the 1720s–40s; the art style that perfectly shows the effect upon a religious sensibility of the concurrently occurring Death of God. The real and the illusory are mixed. The effect is surreal, dream-like, but in its own way hauntingly beautiful. I implore the reader to go and see two of the most astoundingly beautiful interiors in all Europe, Steinhausen and Vierzenheiligen. Our new religion has got to be a religion that helps us to live and say Yes to life in a world as beautiful, precarious and wonky as that; a world in which the utterly transient be-ing of the most short-lived insect fills us with love; so much so that it makes me feel ready to die.

Don't, whatever happens, allow yourself to be drawn back into the kind of fundamentalism that tries to recapture the old dogmatic Reality. The fundamentalist is, and half knows he or she is, a damned soul. Stick to mortal beauty: let it pass, and pass away with it.

9

Solarity

There are very few ancient buildings on Hong Kong Island, but the city does boast a few Buddhist temples, probably of early nineteenth-century origin. They look small, dusty, and very picturesque. The visitor who likes Buddhism heads for them eagerly – and is grievously disappointed. Spiralling 'moon tiger' incense burners smoke quietly in the darkness, and one or two of the crudely carved stone figures may perhaps be Buddhas. But the only current activity of which there is any sign at all is fortune telling: chiefly divination by casting sticks. The visitor who is familiar with dozens of the sutras, and with a few of the principal Buddhist philosophers, is shocked to discover that on the ground in some of its old native lands only the barest trace of Buddhism remains. The Chinese are a life-loving people, and temples like Man Mo do contain sets of the 60 year-gods. (There was one to manage each year of your life, 60 being all you would need.) There is perhaps just enough here for one to be able to imagine a revival of interest in Daoism. But Buddhism is too far gone to be revivable – here, at least.

Could Christianity in the West have become equally corrupt and decadent? Man Mo temple contains no ancient Buddhist literature, and hardly any writing, whereas of course Christian worship does still include reading from the earliest surviving Christian literature. While the New Testament is still read at all, Christianity surely cannot lose touch with itself . . . can it?

Yes, it can. The New Testament does indeed (just about) remember the original message of Jesus. There is a good summary of it in Mark 1.15:

The time is fulfilled, and the kingdom of God is at hand; repent, and believe in the Gospel.

Paraphrasing this, and putting it into our vocabulary, we get something like the following:

Ever since the time of Moses, we have lived under the discipline of religious Law, and under the authority of its teachers and interpreters. We have seen this life of ours as being merely a preparatory period of discipline, to be endured for the sake of a promised time of liberation, yet to come. On that Day, a new radically internalized religion of the heart will replace the organized, institutional, mediated religion that has chafed us for so long. We will feel free: that is, our outpouring emotive life will be able to flow unrepressed. We will be able to live *wholeheartedly*.

Now, at last, the time has come. The last age of the world is beginning, and it is time to start living the last kind of life in a world that neither has nor needs any further world beyond it. We'll need to change our lives: we must stop valuing everything in life solely in terms of whether it will improve our chances of final salvation hereafter. We must give up thinking always in terms of *instrumental* value, and start thinking only in terms of *intrinsic* value. In addition, we must give up all the reactive 'negative' emotions and every kind of *ressentiment*, and begin living from the heart, pouring out ourselves into our lives as generously as we can. We must go way beyond all merely human ideas of justice, which (frankly) function chiefly to cloak a lust for retaliation and revenge.

Those who have learnt to use their eyes will know that the loveliest things in life are the most transient, and the more we are able to love, and to enter into, and identify ourselves with that utter transience of everything, the more we will find that to lose our selves in the love of life is to gain eternal happiness. Everything pours out and passes away, and we should go along with that. Live now, live by dying of love, and know eternal happiness.

The message is platitudinous. At its core, it always is: but it remains, as it always has been, hard to live out in full. But if in these matters there is any truth, it is this. Solarity is everything. It requires us to abandon the idea of the soul as an immortal substance; but then, the Jews did not have that idea. For them we are transient flesh, occasionally touched by Spirit.

Unfortunately, Jesus' message meant the end of organized religion, the end of religious Law, and the end of the need for a privileged class of religious professionals. It also meant, by implication, the end of all supernatural belief; for when God is fully internalized within the heart, the whole supernatural order disappears, being replaced by a purely immanent ethical mysticism of life.

Fyodor Dostoevsky's famous chapter called 'The Grand Inquisitor' in *The Brothers Karamazov* explains with great imaginative clarity why the original Jesus was, and always must be, rejected outright by the official leaders of the very religion whose fulfilment he announced. Of course he was a blasphemer who came to 'abolish the Law'; of course he was a dangerous heretic who threatened to lead the people of Israel astray; and of course he must be put down ruthlessly. So he was, and that's that. We know surprisingly little about the life of Jesus, the Gospels that have reached us being largely mythical creations that picture what Jesus' life *ought to* have been like in the light of later theologies, rather than what it actually *was* like. All we can say is that Jesus of Nazareth, son of Mary and Joseph, and brother of James and others, was a Galilean-Jewish itinerant teacher who travelled around Palestine for a year or two around AD 30, before being executed as a troublemaker. The sources, which are otherwise very diverse, are unanimous in their insistence that he attracted a popular following, but was found extremely objectionable by religious professionals. The tradition of his teaching was very extensively revised and corrupted by his own professed followers, almost from the first. But we can make out the general *tendenz* of the revision process, and that enables us to work backwards and pick out a cluster of early sayings. They broadly confirm that Jesus taught that the Last World was arriving, and that we need to start living its proper life. The older supernaturalist and institutionally mediated kind of religion was now outdated. Jesus was an early teacher of an immediate and markedly humanitarian religion of the heart; and this *was* 'the life of the world to come': a life of pure feeling with absolutely no ill feeling.

Within 20 years the original message was almost wholly lost. The little community went back by a whole dispensation, back to living under apostolic authority, under a law of faith (*regula fidei*), looking away from this world and up to a supernatural world from which the now-risen Jesus would return in glory. They had retreated from the Last World to the penultimate world. Instead of living beatitude now, they were beginning to purify themselves and to hope for personal salvation at the end of time.

Jesus himself had to be completely transformed in order to perform his new function. Instead being the old disobedient and rebellious Son of God, he was completely rewritten as Christ the only-begotten and always perfectly obedient Son of God who desires only to do the will of his heavenly Father. The strain of rewriting Jesus in this way is revealed in the New Testament by the curious *aporia* that surrounds the figure of Lucifer, the Morning Star, and the puzzling closeness of Christ to Satan that survives in Latin theology to this day.

At any rate, the transformation of Jesus into the exemplary, obedient Son of God, the Divine Christ, has been very interestingly reversed in the modern period, in the thought of writers such as Milton, Blake and Nietzsche. We begin to understand the tragedy of the Church, of which today many Church leaders are obviously aware. Jesus' followers felt that his message had to survive. To survive, it must become embodied in an institution that can live on in different cultures and different historical periods. The institution needs leaders, it needs authority, it needs a mystique of its own, and it needs a Law of faith. So it was and is unavoidable that Jesus' message should be able to reach us only in very highly corrupted form. Jesus preached the Kingdom, solar living; what we got was the *Codex Iuris Canonicae*, and a glorious tradition of sacred art in which Jesus always looks a bit pained, silent and withdrawn . . . in fact he always looks as if he wishes he were somewhere else. Indeed, he really *should* be somewhere else: he doesn't belong here. And Jesus' own acute discomfort is mirrored by that of the modern educated Church leader. As a leader, he is institutionally obliged to take the line that will keep the peace among the faithful; but he wouldn't have got to be the leader unless he were sufficiently educated to know better. So he (or she, nowadays) is stuck in untruth, forced to draw a clear distinction between what his official position obliges him to say, and what as a private individual he knows to be the truth. Historical constraints have made the Church into a body whose leaders are forced into a position of compulsory untruth for which they must pay a heavy personal price. Depression, alas.

However, the Churches of all denominations, and indeed the institutions of other faiths too, are nowadays in irreversible decline. Suppose we ask the question: is it possible, at this late date, to reform and renew the best features of the Christian tradition?

Yes, by studying and responding to the call of the original Jesus. If we want to do this *from within* Christianity's official legacy, we'll have to show in detail how and why the two most influential modern New Testament scholars, namely Albert Schweitzer and Rudolf Bultmann, got their answers to these questions badly wrong. As for the Churches, they'll have to study the Quakers in order to learn how they might transform themselves into a working modern post-ecclesiastical religious society. It could conceivably be done, but I doubt very much if it *will* be done.

Alternatively, there could be a rediscovery and revival of the core message in popular culture, quite independently of the Churches. This can easily be envisaged, and did actually happen in 'the Sixties'. Hippiedom, flower power, Give peace a chance! The Christ-figure of the age was John Lennon. Eventually, he assumed much of the popular iconography of Christ: he came to *look* like Jesus. But however that may be, Sixties popular culture at its height, going with the flow and saying that love is all you need, was much closer to the original Jesus than the Church is ever likely to get.

This suggests a third possibility. We may perhaps conclude that the core message of Jesus does not actually *need* any enduring institutional embodiment. It may not need even the *name* of Jesus.

Plato lives on, 1,500 years or so after his original Academy was shut down; and Christian humanitarian values, solar living, and an extravertive mystical love of all things transient will probably survive better if they are left *without* institutional backing. Every academy always ends by getting it all wrong, whereas outside the academy *Magna est veritas, et prevalebit.*

PART TWO

Epistles

10

A New Method of Religious Enquiry

On 7 July 2005, four suicide bombers attacked Central London, causing explosions on Underground trains and on a bus that killed over 50 people. One of the victims was a youngish man of about 38 years, who was a deacon in the Baptist church to which he belonged. Giving media interviews afterwards, his friends spoke about their grief, saying that they planned a service that would be 'a celebration of his life'. He, they said, was someone who had 'loved life and lived it to the full'.

Here is a neat example of the way in which we modern Western people currently profess two very different religions. Like the friends of that Baptist deacon who was so prematurely struck down, when we are in church, in a traditional religious setting, we still preserve intact the vocabulary of our ancestral faith – Protestant, Catholic, Jewish or whatever. It seems that we don't want it to be diluted in any way. But when we are using ordinary language in a public setting the old distinctively Christian vocabulary is no longer usable, and we find ourselves employing instead an entirely different vocabulary, the vocabulary of the new religion of life. It seems that we have two different religions at once, without recognizing it.

When I first discovered this strange fact, I made one or two other odd discoveries. The emergent new religion of life was first spelled out really simply and vividly by Tolstoy, near the end of *War and Peace*: 'Life is everything, Life is God, and to love life is to love God.' Various writers, such as Nietzsche and D. H. Lawrence, have developed these ideas. But the religion of life only became built into our everyday speech during the decades since

World War Two. Today, it is dominant: as Osama bin Laden once correctly remarked, he and his associates love death, whereas we Westerners are lovers of life.

I became involved with these ideas in the late 1990s, when I was collecting stock phrases that are current in ordinary language, with a view to finding out from them what ordinary people currently think about questions of philosophy, religion and ethics. My findings astonished me. Ordinary language, it seems, has already done the job of radical theology. It has radically secularized the main themes of Christian doctrine, bringing the entire supernatural world down into the ongoing flow of human cultural and historical life, and so converting the old relation between the soul and God into the new relation between *my* life and the stream of life as a whole that has brought me to life, and that now demands my commitment. In hundreds of vivid idioms that everyone knows and uses, we reveal our conviction that the religious object is now just life itself, transient, precious, sacred, sometimes seemingly cruel and always finite. We must each of us assume full responsibility for the conduct of our own lives. We must each of us live our own life in our own way, trying to make, each of us, our own distinctive contribution to the whole, and trying each of us to find the faith and the courage to say Yes to life with all our hearts until life comes to an end for us.

That is the religion to which we have quite recently, but demonstrably, become committed by our own everyday speech. It may perhaps be seen as having been foreshadowed in the eschatological dreams of Christianity, of Marxism, and of figures such as John Lennon and Martin Luther King Jr., who all looked forward to a time when everyday life on this earth would have become so filled with religious value and dignity that it would fully satisfy our hearts. At that time, the old Protestant turn to everyday life in this world would reach its final consummation in a universal, this-worldly religious humanism.

Great: but people have reacted with caution and suspicion to my claim that I have reached such a momentous theological conclusion merely by a straightforward empirical study of the way ordinary language has recently been developing. They smell a rat. Something is wrong. To social scientists it seems obvious that in modern Western societies religion is extremely diverse. How can I claim that facts about ordinary language show that beneath all this superficial diversity there is a single modern religion of life that involves us all?

To allay these doubts, I need to spell out my claims more fully and accurately.

I have been promising that the new method of religious enquiry will be genuinely objective and empirical, and free from the dominance of traditional theological assumptions. Well, you may say, there is nothing very original or surprising about that. The empirical study of religion, a cluster of embryonic subjects, has been around for a long time. For more than a century – and at least since the time of William James – people have been expressing the hope that the study of religion would soon be established on a sound scientific basis.

How was this to be done? Studying religion would presumably begin with measuring human religiosity by various criteria. One might find out by polling, for example, what religious beliefs people profess to hold and what religious practices they claim to engage in. Having established people's degree of religiosity on various indices, one might then ask how religiosity varies with age, sex, political allegiance, social class, mental health, education and so on. When interesting-looking correlations are found, we then devise theories to explain them, and try to think of ways to test the theories. All this could be done with the main emphasis either upon individual psychology (the psychology of religion), or upon people in general (the social psychology of religion), or upon the working of social institutions (the sociology of religion). To check people's personal claims about their own behaviour, one might also conduct a 'direct count' of the numbers of people who (for example) attend services at places of worship on holy days. If we then compare people's claims with the figures we have obtained by direct counting we are soon reminded of a great truth: when they are being questioned by a serious-looking person holding a pen and a clipboard people will always double their church attendance, just as they always halve their alcohol consumption.

That is a giveaway. It reveals the limitations of social psychology as it has usually been conducted so far, and shows why its findings are not very interesting. Ordinary people, when they are questioned, instantly guess that they are being checked up on to see how closely they conform to official standards. So they obligingly give, not a strictly accurate answer, but an answer bent somewhat in the direction of what (they take it) the questioner wants to hear.

What has gone wrong is that the academic researchers have almost always seen their topic and framed their questions from the point of view of the religious establishment. Although social scientists have always had a reputation for being inclined to the Left, the fact is that academics as such are followers of Plato: they see the world from the point of view of the ruling group. They have always asked how far the people hold the beliefs that the establishment thinks they *ought* to hold, and how far they do the things that the establishment thinks they *ought* to be doing. Thus the academics have hitherto been measuring not people's religiosity but merely their *conformity*. It has simply been assumed that the locally dominant religious institutions and traditions occupy the high ground, and have the right to dictate the agenda and to formulate the questions. You are religious to the extent that you conform to the standards they set. Accordingly, researchers in Christian countries have asked great numbers of people: Do you believe in a personal God? Do you believe in, or have you ever been conscious, of a higher power outside ourselves? Do you believe that Jesus is the Son of God? Do you believe in the Devil? – and the replies to such questions are taken to indicate how religious people are. But, I suggest, we have very good reason to think that when they are questioned in such a way about such matters, people tend to return the answers that (as they think) the questioner wants to hear, and secondly, we also have very good reason to think that people's real religious interest nowadays lies elsewhere. Unfortunately, the social scientists usually found it difficult to ask themselves in a genuinely open-minded manner: 'What is the *actual* religion of the people? What do they *really* think?'

The obvious response to this is that we need definitions of religion, indices of religiosity and so on that are objective, and not biased in favour of any particular institution, or creed, or culture. In addition, we have to find a way round the 'reflexivity' problem which arises when the people we are studying recognize that they are under the microscope and modify their behaviour accordingly. Here we will need something analogous to the blind-testing of pharmaceuticals: we need something that will not *know* that we are looking at it.

I have a twofold reply to these points. In the first place, religious naturalism of the sort that I propose (and have recently discussed in *The Way to Happiness* (2005) is exceptional in that it should be capable of developing and testing a general, rational theory of what religion is, how it works, why it is a good thing and how and why it evolves. Such a body of theory might simply replace traditional theology and apologetics. Secondly, the material that we shall study is simply ordinary language. The vernacular is a very large, complex living system in which we all participate, to which we all contribute, and which we all know quite remarkably thoroughly. It is on the whole very well-documented, and it already has built into it what I shall call our common valuations of things (CV), our popular philosophy (PP), and our popular religious philosophy of life (PRPL). And it is available for objective study: we can watch it changing as the times change.

In the literature of Religious Studies and the sociology of religion it is often stressed how very plural the bigger Western countries have become in modern times. Thus in contemporary Britain some nine or ten 'world religions' are established, with many of them divided into dozens, or even (in the case of Christianity) hundreds of distinct sects. In addition, scholars who have attempted to list them have recorded about 1,500 new religious movements (NRMs). This certainly gives an impression of enormous diversity, and may make some people wonder how far there can be a genuinely common PRPL. But when we study ordinary language – and especially when we collect and examine the striking and vivid stock phrases that play such a large part in everyday speech – we discover to our surprise that there really *is* a coherent and interesting PRPL. It is demonstrably there, in the language. Indeed, I would go a little further, and claim that in the first Life-book I have already done enough to establish the existence of a new religion, the religion of life, which has in the past half-century become socially established. Every one of us knows it, and every one of us from time to time voices bits of it. We are remarkably widely and deeply agreed about it. Thus the new method of religious enquiry is capable of showing people a whole new religion in which they already believe, and whose language they are already talking. It often happens that we discover ourselves to have been saying much more than we have yet realized, but this is the most startling instance of the phenomenon that I have met.

We can now present in outline the general theoretical framework or setting within which the new method is used.

Through our language we shape ourselves, our social relations, and the common world in which we live. But we don't create everything, absolutely. Language's Other, the raw material that it struggles to shape into an orderly, habitable world, may be called Be-ing – or perhaps, because it is not itself within language, we should write it as Being. It is an efflux of formless contingency, gentle but wayward and not completely masterable. This obscure element of unmasterability or resistance, which is not directly capturable in our thought or language, is often alluded to in periphrases or euphemisms. Ordinary language knows it best as 'it', as in **Face up to it**, and **Don't let it get you down.**

Our human life is therefore always subject to certain permanent conditions or limits, within which we must live. Minimally, they include temporality, contingency and finitude – or, in more popular speech, Time, Chance and Death. We always live in time, we are always vulnerable to happenstance and misfortune, and our life is always bounded – by finitude, and ultimately by death.

I don't follow tradition by calling these limits 'metaphysical'. They may simply be thought of as very general facts of life, so general that we often think that, in these respects at least, we cannot clearly imagine how our life could be otherwise.

The three conditions or limits are the polar opposites, in Platonism, of eternity, necessity and infinity – three metaphysical attributes of God. And our subjection to them is what Leibniz in his *Theodicée* (1716) calls 'metaphysical evil'. Slavoj Žižek has interestingly argued that in modern times – and especially since the work of F. W. J. von Schelling (1775–1854) – as attention has switched from the eternal world to this world, so the three conditions have come to set the agenda for modern thought.

The three conditions, or limits, are modes of finite Be-ing. In the past, people have often fancied that we might perhaps be delivered from them – for example, in a heavenly world to be entered after our deaths. But that now seems very doubtful. Being without temporality is just as hard to imagine as language without time. So it seems better simply to concentrate on the task of recognizing and coming to terms with the three conditions. We do this by elaborating symbolic representations of them and stories about them, and evolving social rituals by means of which we negotiate with them. The result is what people call *religion*.

Religion is a highly self-involving activity. In science we are trained to set aside our own subjectivity, and in large areas of philosophy, too, the self is far from prominent. But in religion we always test out, test the disposition of, the unknown otherness by venturing our selves and our own lives. It is at this point that religion and art are closest to each other. I put forward and I commit my whole self and my whole life in the attempt to relate myself to and find some way of dealing with the mysterious conditions that circumscribe my life – and the even darker Otherness that hovers behind them. In the past, we used to work by personifying the conditions, and then trying to deal with them on a person-to-person basis. More recently, as our understanding of the human condition has moved towards what I call 'Empty radical humanism', we have tried simply to identify them and learn to live with them in a way that **makes the best of things**. Boldest of all is the all-out attempt radically to *revalue* contingency, temporality and finitude – my own favourite, ultra-Nietzschean strategy.

In ordinary language there are various totalizing words and expressions that we use by way of referring to **all this**. Such terms include **life, things, everything, it all, it, fate, luck, destiny, God, the nature of things, someone up there, the lap of the gods** and so on. A simple count of the number of fresh and lively idioms currently available to us in ordinary language under each of these heads indicates that, of all these expressions, **life, it** and **it all** are today the most important. For example, in ordinary (English) language today there are only about 25–28 God idioms still current, whereas there are at least 200 religiously significant life idioms, almost all of which have come into popular use only in the past two generations. **Life** is at present the most popular totalizing word, by using which we invoke the conditions and our human situation as a whole. **Life** has by far the richest cloud of idioms. (**It** idioms may be even more numerous, but they are somewhat less vivid imaginatively.)

During the twentieth century an enormous growth in communications has ensured that we all hear a great deal of our own language every day, and from very varied sources. We have become highly sensitive to idioms. The result, so far largely unremarked by scholars, is that the everyday speech of ordinary people has become highly 'intertextual'. We talk in quotes, in highly contagious stock phrases that have spread very quickly from mouth to mouth. By way of illustration, I urge the reader to examine and consider the extraordinary rapidity with which vivid, much-needed new idioms such as **lifestyle** (from c.1972–3), and **Get a life!** (1988–9) were able to spread around the world, utterly indifferent to the physical distances between the USA, Britain, Australia and other English-speaking countries. Indeed, the two idioms just mentioned have easily jumped from English into many other languages.

We can safely assume that if a new idiom quickly catches on, spreads across the English-speaking world and becomes a part of the language, then it does so because it meets a real need. It says in a smart and pithy way something that great numbers of people often find themselves wanting to say. It does a good job. More generally, every bit of ordinary language has been very thoroughly tested and refined in the toughest laboratory of all, that of the street and the marketplace. Our language is a living, evolving organism, in which mutations are being introduced and a process of natural selection goes on constantly, and its condition today is by far the best and most reliable index of what the people themselves actually think today. We are what we say. And notice that in being active members of a language group who trade words with others all the time, we are generating and revising the PRPL continually.

This discussion indicates the criteria for regarding an idiom – for example, about life – as being *religiously significant*. In itself, life is not a distinct thing. It is simply the going on of our social existence. But in some life idioms very bold metaphors are used in connection with life. It may be objectified, or even personified. Dispositions may be attributed to it, and we may be spoken of as having dealings with it. Sometimes traditional religious language is transferred to life. Where some of these features are present, they are present for a reason – a religious reason. Their conspicuousness is intended to catch our attention, and provoke thought. The new method involves a systematic attempt to collect and interpret them – and especially to pick out new ones, whose meaning is still fresh and vivid.

In its basic structure – the parts of speech, grammar and syntax, sentence structure – ordinary language both reflects and prescribes (arguably, it just *is*) the popular philosophy (PP). Our basic world view is the one our language gives us. And, of course, in its basic structure ordinary language changes only slowly.

Sometimes, however, a small shift in idiom may indicate that a major philosophical change is taking place. For example, during the past twenty years the word 'perception', which used to mean the mere impressing of sense data upon our sense organs, and therefore seemed to be theory-neutral, has come instead to be used to mean 'interpretation'. The implication of the new usage is that over a wide range of social and political questions 'the facts' are never pure: our apprehension of them from the first involves interpretation. Thus the new use of 'perception' to mean 'interpretation' signals an important philosophical shift away from our traditional British Empiricism. Contrary to what is usually supposed, ordinary people are not without philosophy. Even one small shift in linguistic usage may be enough to prove the point.

Religious change shows itself in the language in a rather similar way. We are not talking about changes in basic linguistic structures, but about piquant, provocative new idioms that deliberately draw our attention to a significant change in religious attitudes and valuations. Phrases like **wrestling with life, loving life, tempting life,** and **having faith in life** must have puzzled people at first – until they saw the obvious, which is that standard phrases about God have here been *consciously* transferred to life. A change is being *flagged*. We are being told to think about life, just about our own daily existence, as we used to think of God. We are being advised to cope with life by reifying it, by personifying it, attributing dispositions to it, and taking up religious attitudes towards it. We do this, and the idioms multiply. Then we hesitate, and remind ourselves that **life is what we make it.** Thus when we collect and study the life idioms current today we are studying at first hand the true popular religion of today, a this-worldly and immediate religion just of life. And the idioms also show us actively debating this new religion even as we adopt it.

If we study the great religious traditions in the very large number of their current sectarian forms, plus the NRMs currently established in our society, together with the various degrees and forms of agnosticism, scepticism and unbelief, we may get the impression of a cultural world that has become very highly pluralistic. But when we study religious thought going on in the idioms of ordinary language we are taught the opposite lesson. At the deepest level (for nothing is deeper than ordinary language) – at the deepest level there is a very high degree of unanimity. The ordinary person in the street outside may know little or nothing about Sikhs or scientologists, but she knows all the life idioms and has probably herself used many of them. The *SOED* entry s.v. 'life' tells us with brilliant clarity and economy what *everybody* knows about life; and the same would still be true if we were to expand the *OED* entry to incorporate all of the several hundred life idioms (religious and other) that are currently to be found in daily use. Ordinary language, huge and complex though it is, is what everybody knows very well, and the religious changes currently going on in it are changes that are currently going on in every English-speaking person. And I should add here that the same is true of the other European languages of which I have a smattering. I am not talking only about English.

Wittgenstein and his followers have made us familiar with the idea of the centrality and importance of ordinary language and the world view to which it commits us – a basic common world view that we must always presuppose and can never entirely escape. But they never did the research to establish in detail exactly *what* philosophical, religious and ethical ideas our ordinary language gives us, and they have almost nothing to say about how religious language evolves historically. Wittgenstein seems never to have regarded linguistic change as being philosophically interesting. But, I am saying, the case of the life idioms, which proliferated so much during the course of the twentieth century, gives us direct access to major religious change as it is actually occurring. We can document precisely and in detail the birth and the diffusion of new religious ideas as it is proceeding, not in remote cultural settings, but among ourselves and in our own time.

From all these considerations I conclude that we have here the basis for a new method of studying religion. By examining ordinary language, and especially current idioms, we can quickly and easily establish empirically, and at the deepest and most general level, what the real religion of ordinary people currently is, and how it is changing.

I personally accept the main theses of religious naturalism. I think that because we humans are the only makers of our language, we must also be the only makers of religion, and that by studying people's language we can quite easily teach ourselves to observe the genesis and diffusion of new religious sentiments and ideas. But even if you disagree with me, even if you are an adherent of some form of supernatural faith, you will still presumably agree that religion has a *human* history, and that we can write that history on the basis of the things that people in the past have said and written.

Use of the new method suggests a few theses about the nature of religious change, and – more interestingly – why there has to be religious change at all.

1 Religious change very often involves disruption of the received distinction between things sacred and things profane, or unclean. The line between them may be drawn in a new place, as when something hitherto regarded as 'unclean' or 'profane' is deliberately and combatively revalued and declared to be holy after all. Alternatively, by a grand utopian or 'Kingdom' gesture the line may be effaced altogether, as when 'all foods' are declared clean, or 'everything that lives' is called holy.

2 Religious change may involve an iconoclastic attack upon an overgrown and overbearing apparatus of religious mediation that too often becomes itself the religious object, and exploits the believer, rather than linking him to the Sacred. Thus the woman mystic of early Islam, Rabia, refuses to be discouraged by the custom of excluding women from public worship. She has God in her heart, and therefore has no need to suppose that she could get any nearer to God either by entering a particular building, or by turning to face Mecca. By saying which Rabia points out that the apparatus of religious mediation always in effect *finitizes* God, in a way that official theology declares to be absurd. The same strategy, of sardonically cutting official religion down by turning it against itself to produce a paradox, is still common in modern English idiom. Compare 'Reverend Lovejoy' in *The Simpsons*, saying consolingly that 'God loves his victims'. In summary, one may say that iconoclastic assaults upon the apparatus of religious mediation as being old, obstructive and absurd are typical means by which today we are making the transition to the new and more immediate kind of religion.

3 In the most extreme case, traditional religious institutions and language may have become very decayed. The doctrines and the moral teaching may be discredited, and the metaphors may be stale. In such a time it may be that the old vocabulary has to be dropped, and new metaphors must be minted to revive religious

thought and feeling. The only form that true religion can take is that of pure creative religious thought.

My own studies of religious thought in everyday speech have suggested to me that we now live in such a time. The traditional vocabulary has become badly decayed. The new popular religion of life does represent a very bold attempt to make a fresh start, and the fact that it has so quickly become so well-established in the language is a good reason for taking it very seriously indeed. It is already established and constraining us. You don't realize, but you do already believe it. You are already *confessing* it.

But is it actually *true*? And, in general, can the method of religious enquiry that I am proposing promise to deliver any substantive religious truths? Traditional supernatural religion involves – more, it openly confesses that it *depends* upon – the meaningfulness and the truth of claims about how things are in a supernatural world that is quite distinct from the ordinary life-world in which ordinary language has its home. Where that is the situation, it seems pretty clear that, in a strong sense, the major claims of Christianity must be either true or false or meaningless. But the new religion of life that we now find embedded in our everyday speech makes no metaphysical or quasi-factual claims. It seems that all we can say of it is, in Wittgenstein's words, 'This language game is played!' People actively *want* to say these things and to take up these attitudes: they feel it does them good.

When we are studying ordinary language and its idioms, the old 'strong' kind of truth – metaphysical, categorical or 'dogmatic' truth – is out of place. But don't worry: there never really was any of it, anyway. We should be very content to limit ourselves to 'weak' truth. In the weak sense, the religion of life is true religion. It teaches us to value life as highly as it can be valued, and to enjoy life as much as it can be enjoyed. What more could you ask for? There isn't anything more. That's non-realism: for as you will remember from (1–4) above, there is no ready-made intelligible cosmos out there. There is only the outpouring formless, contingent flux of Be-ing, and us, and our language, which is the tool we use in our unending struggle to build an agreed, formed, habitable, objective common human world to live in. It follows that we can no longer make the old distinction between our construction of the world and the way the world is objectively and apart from us. We have, and we see, only our world. It follows that there is for us only our present truth, which is the religious truth that the new method exposes.

11

What's the Point of It All?

Writing in the late 1880s, Nietzsche suddenly pauses and says to himself: 'What a lot of nineteenth centuries there are, waiting to be described by historians in the future!' He has recognized that modern society is so large-scale, so hugely productive and destructive, and containing so many conflicting forces, that many, many different interpretations of it are always possible. We never reach a final view about its worth, or in what direction it is all heading.

The ambiguity persists. There always have been, and there still are, both people for whom the Victorian age was a period of great moral assurance, energetic, confident and expansionist, and also people for whom the whole period was clouded by anxiety and depression over the loss of religious faith, 'the decline of the West', and looming nihilism.

Now that we are in a position to look back on it, the twentieth century presents us with all the same difficulties in even more acute form. On the one hand, it was by far the most productive period human beings have known. As average life expectancy in a country such as this one rose during the nineteenth century from around 28 to 48 years, so during the twentieth century it rose again, from around 48 to 78 years, with enormous increases in the availability to all of easy access to cultural resources, and cheap transport and communications. Adding in great advances in medicine and public health, the average life has become far longer, more prosperous and culturally richer than ever before. Yet at the same time the twentieth was also much the most destructive century, ravaged by the decline of religion and the clash of violent secular political ideologies, and severely threatened by overpopulation and degradation of the environment. Even more than the nineteenth, the twentieth century has seen a constant storm of change, and a continuous controversy between optimistic and pessimistic interpretations of what's been happening and where we are all heading.

Some things in the late twentieth century were quite new. After about 1950, the whole of cultural life was increasingly guided by the mass media. After about 1960, the transmission of culture, faith and values through the family and religious institutions almost ceased, and instead young people came to draw their world view and their values from the media in general, and from pop music in particular. The resulting 'detraditionalization' has accelerated the decline of traditional religion. During the early 1980s, the ring of communications satellites around the world became complete and fully reliable, so that money, ideas, entertainment and talk began to be traded continuously in a single world-wide conversation of humanity. Everyone who travels widely notices that, especially in the great cities, the conversational agenda has become much the same everywhere.

Paradoxically, this continuous global exchange is not producing any unchallenged world-wide consensus. On the contrary, its most obvious effect so far has been to provoke a violent ethno-nationalist and religious backlash from various groups of people who feel that they are not being invited to the party. Which brings me to another paradox: the flood of information that reaches all of us every day seems to be making us not more settled in our opinions but more volatile, and we must all of us be aware of having quietly abandoned views that only a few decades ago were accepted by everyone as obvious truths.

For example, 30 years ago everyone was still Malthusian. We were all threatened by a catastrophic population explosion: but today almost half the world is threatened by declining fertility, and some European countries are being told that they now face really alarming depopulation. Thirty years ago 'the secularization thesis' was still in the saddle, and people supposed that as knowledge grew and technology advanced the whole culture must become more secular, so that organized religion would fade away and generally cease to be a problem. But today religion is back with a vengeance, transformed into new and very militant political ideologies such as Zionism, Islamism and BJP Hinduism. No religion, not even Buddhism, is exempt from this extreme form of politicization: in Sri Lanka the national mythology of the Sinhala people assures them that the Buddha gave Ceylon to them, to be occupied by them alone, and – amazingly – Buddhist monks have endorsed their government's war against the Tamils. There can be little doubt that in this new form religion will cause quite as much mayhem in the twenty-first century as the secular political ideologies of fascism and communism caused in the twentieth century. What seems to have happened in that fascism and communism have bequeathed their aggressive messianism back to the religions from which they first drew it. By a horrible irony, modern religion has been back-poisoned by a corrupt version of itself. The long-term result will probably be that humanity in general will some day reject messianic fundamentalist religion just as decisively as we have already rejected fascism and communism.

One last example of the way long-held assumptions are nowadays liable to sudden reversal: since the Enlightenment we have believed that the historical process in which we are caught up is generally characterized by a steady long-term advance, both of knowledge and of personal freedom. An educated and fully participant liberal democracy is the End of history, at least in the sense of being the *Telos*, the goal of history. But a decade ago the sudden debate about the ideas of Francis Fukuyama may have marked the beginning of a sharp reversal. In an article called 'Post-democracy',[1] the leading liberal philosopher Richard Rorty said regretfully that he feared that the golden age of bourgeois liberal democracy is now coming to an end. It lasted 200 years, and it was good while it lasted, but we cannot afford it any longer. People are nowadays being easily persuaded to surrender their freedoms in the interests of 'homeland

---

1 Richard Rorty, 'Post-Democracy', *London Review of Books*, 1 April 2004.

security'. Thoroughgoing, magnificently 'easy', American-style liberal democracy is no longer practicable in the new age of suicide bombers, economic vulnerability, and the looming spectre of the breakdown of the state. The model for the future will be the limited and centrally 'guided' democracy of Putin's Russian Federation, and of countries like, perhaps, China and Singapore. Real democratic freedom we can't afford any more: it's too vulnerable to attack. But most of us will doubtless be perfectly content with homeland security and 'guided' democracy rather than freedom – even in America.

All these alarming reversals and new ideas have emerged only during the last few years, and they show us how difficult the task of the religious thinker has recently become. It is harder than ever to reach and to hold any settled view of the rapidly shifting times in which we live – times in which there is no stable truth, and the prevailing consensus about the direction in which we are all going is liable to such sudden and unexpected reversals. For about 200 years (that is, since about the time of Schopenhauer), people have made the point by remarking that the basic facts of life and the current state of the world may be the same for the optimist and the pessimist. But without falsifying or denying any of the facts the two end up by producing wildly different interpretations of what it all means, for them, and for us; and often we can't find any simple test that will help us to decide which of them is right.

Do you see how acute the problem is? The optimist and the pessimist both take account of all the facts, and both are rational. But they produce flatly opposed visions of the overall human condition, and we cannot find any agreed and reliable criterion for deciding which of them is right. This is very bad for religious thought, because traditionally religious thought has always needed and has always started from just such a big, overall, global picture and diagnosis of the human situation. In times as unstable and ambivalent as ours, I am saying, how can religious thought hope to find an agreed starting point? Until we can form a settled view about where we are and where things are heading, religious thought cannot show us why and how we should re-orient our lives. Anyway, there is a case for saying that 'the state of the world' and 'the human condition' are simply too ambiguous and vague for it to be possible to make true general statements about them.

I used to think I could deal with this problem. During the 1980s, I still felt pretty confident of the permanent and in-all-situations goodness and religious efficacy of Christian myths, symbols and moral values. It seemed enough simply to argue for the legitimacy of a non-realist interpretation of them. Otherwise, things could go on after the end of metaphysics without any very painful change; and indeed during the 1980s, people did often remark with surprise that *in my practice* I remained a rather traditional Anglican Christian. But by the mid-1990s I had come to feel that I must give up officiating in the Church, and must move to a much more radical position.

It is this recent move to a much more radical outlook that I have to discuss today. I shall summarize the change in three slogans. The first is as follows: *The decline of dogmatic belief leads to the return of the great questions.*

The traditional religious believer usually lived in a very *full* world, and felt himself to be at the centre of cosmic attention. To put the point in environmental terms, places like the Canadian Arctic and the Australian outback may seem to a modern Westerner to be fearsomely empty and barren: but to their native inhabitants, the Inuit and the Aborigine, the same places are teeming with spirits and stories. Their respective worlds are to them rich and homely, and they know just what to do and how to live there. The Inuit is *at home* in the Arctic, and getting plenty of help and guidance. The Aborigine can survive in places where white men die of thirst. And now to make the same point in psychological terms: the conservative Evangelical Protestant who reads Scripture every day and communes with the Lord all the time also lives in a very rich and busy mental world. His head is full of thoughts about what God is, what God has done for him, what is God's will for his life, how he can bear witness to God's saving grace, and so on. For him, all the Great Questions of Life are simply solved. He's quite convinced that he knows all the answers. Historically, Jews, Christians and Muslims have often claimed that a really good education in their Scriptures is a *complete* education. It is all one needs; and I suggest that the explanation for this seemingly extravagant claim lies in the way that strong dogmatic religious faith seems to fill one's head, fill one's world, and answer all questions. The believer thinks that the entire supernatural world is gathered in a big circle above him, looking down at what he's doing with intense interest, and giving him non-stop commentary, support and advice. He is in the centre. He just couldn't be more important. When you are in that position, of course you are confident that you do understand what life is all about. It's about your moral action, and your journey to salvation.

Then in the seventeenth century there was a violent revolution in the world-picture of Western people. The rich complicated spirit-filled Universe of Dante's *Divine Comedy* – which is still around in, for example, Shakespeare's *The Merchant of Venice*,[2] and which even Milton has not given up[3] – has suddenly been threatened by the work of Galileo and Descartes. A new empty mechanical Universe is replacing the old religious cosmology, and in this new Universe it seems there are to be no spirits, no meaning, no purposes, no values. Human beings are to lose forever the old friendly and supportive cosmologies. We will no longer be able to assume that the world and life are ready-made to make sense to us. This, in the 1650s or so, was a foretaste of what would eventually come to be called 'The Death of God'; and the first person to say what it felt like was Blaise Pascal: 'The eternal silence of those infinite spaces terrifies me.'[4] Suddenly the angels

---

2 *Merchant of Venice*, Act V, Sc. 1: Lorenzo's speech, beginning at 'How sweet the moonlight sleeps upon this bank!'
3 Although Milton had met Galileo and sympathized strongly with his views, the cosmology of *Paradise Lost* (1667) differs from that of Dante only for scriptural, and not for scientific reasons. The new scientific theories are discussed in Book VIII, but they have not yet radically changed Milton's whole world-view.
4 Blaise Pascal, 1670, *Pensées*, trans. J. M. Cohen (Pelican Classics edition), §91. There are still confusingly many different editions, translations and numberings of this text, of course. But every commentator notes the prominence of the theme of

are gone, and the cosmos is an endless barren desert. One feels clear-headed and belief-less, in a silent, empty world.

Apart from a number of passages in Shakespeare's principal tragedies, Pascal is the best early example of the general rule that we are presently discussing. The sudden and very thoroughgoing disenchantment of the world during the seventeenth century inevitably left many gifted individuals feeling that we have become aliens in our own world, and so led to the beginnings of a big revival of the traditional Great Questions. Hence my slogan: the decline of dogmatic belief leads to the return of the great questions. The universe doesn't talk to us any more. It has become cold and enigmatic. The human being feels himself naked and alone before the mysteries of existence.

In later thought, the return of the great questions is particularly apparent in those philosophers who are the most conscious of wanting to return to the beginnings of Western thought, and who best articulate the awe, wonder and dread that the lay person feels in the face of the mystery of existence and the universal human condition: Schopenhauer, Nietzsche, Heidegger. The great questions are also very prominent in the writers who best articulate the great nineteenth-century loss of faith: George Eliot, Mark Rutherford, Thomas Hardy, and A. E. Housman. Here it will be enough to mention two visual artists – Paul Gauguin and Damien Hirst.

In the Museum of Fine Arts at Boston, Massachusetts, is Gauguin's largest painting, done in 1897 towards the end of his troubled, restless life. On the top left hand corner of the canvas Gauguin has written three short sentences in French: *Where do we come from? What are we? Where are we going?* – sentences which give the work its usual title, and show that Gauguin saw his whole life as an artist as having been an attempt to find a satisfactory way of responding to and dealing with the great questions that haunted him. He was a wanderer because there was nowhere in the world that really felt like home to him.

---

the Great Questions in Pascal's thought. Intensely Christian though he is, they worry him as much as they worry A. E. Housman.

In a recent interview Damien Hirst refers to Gauguin's painting, and identifies himself strongly with what Gauguin says:

> There's only ever been one idea in art. You know, the Gauguin questions: Where do we come from? What are we? Where are we going? What's it all about, Alfie?[5]

At first sight the generation of young British artists who came to prominence during the early 1990s, and who included Damien Hirst, Rachel Whiteread, Angus Fairhurst, Ron Mueck, Sarah Lucas, Gary Hume and many others, were aggressively secular. Their work seemed to the public to be anti-beauty, anti-'good taste', and anti-historical. It seemed to be loud, knowing, punk and in-your-face: coarse, confrontational and intimidating. But by now we have become aware of the prominence of traditional religious themes in their work – and by that I mean not only the traditional topics of Latin theology, Eden, the Fall, sinful human nature, the struggle for redemption through suffering, the person of the Redeemer and so on, but *also* the older and more universal great questions: memory, transience, loss, sickness, decline and death – especially death. These are the issues that are said to have driven the young Buddha to begin his quest. Their pedigree in modern art goes back through Gilbert and George and Francis Bacon to German Expressionism, the Fauves, and ultimately Gauguin and Van Gogh; a tradition which like Hardy and Sartre remains obviously religious in one sense even while it is *anti*-religious in another. By that I mean that an atheistic existentialist who is deeply concerned with the tragedy of the human condition may still be a recognizably religious person, and even a very strongly religious person, despite the fact that he rejects Christian theology outright and is militantly atheist. One might cite here the film director Luis Buñuel's famous saying: 'I am an atheist still, thank God!'[6]

---

5 London *Daily Telegraph*, 28 February 2004: from an interview conducted by Martin Gayford, whom I have consulted about the precise wording of my quotation.
6 The only source I have for this oft-quoted *mot* is Ado Kyrou, *Luis Buñuel: An Introduction*, New York: Simon and Schuster, 1963.

That leads me conveniently to my second maxim: *In our age the religious life very often takes the form of a lifelong preoccupation with the Great Questions; and many of us are best able to become ourselves and find ourselves by working out our own personal 'take' on the Great Questions.* Damien Hirst has suggested something of the kind, by hinting that his own art represents his own personal struggle with the questions of the flesh, time, transience, sickness and mortality. He feels chronically and acutely insecure, and puts things in glass cases by way of trying to pin them down and preserve them. And one might say something similar about other people's hobbies and preoccupations. Thus a woman whose life is devoted to creating and maintaining a beautiful garden could by that means be saying something about her own image of Eden, the Earthly Paradise, and about the human struggle to order the world and keep decay, corruption and anarchy at bay. Certainly, for great numbers of English people their house and garden is their own private religion, their consoling personal image of the way things ought to be.

More generally, people reveal their true selves – and as I would say, their deepest religious thoughts – in their ways of dealing with ageing and approaching death. This thought first struck me really forcibly in connection with a small group of literary men that includes Kingsley Amis, Philip Larkin and John Betjeman. All were preoccupied with death, and approached it with the utmost dread and horror. Apparently, death as a religious problem was just the same for the atheist Amis, the agnostic/atheist Larkin, and the Christian Betjeman. They couldn't cope with it at all: and I'm bound to conclude that Betjeman's religion was of no use to him whatever when he finally needed it. Whether it ever occurred to him that there might be a better religious path than camp Anglo-Catholicism, I do not know.

What I *do* know for sure is that ever since the Enlightenment there has been a gradual shifting of the focus of interest from the world above to *this* world, and from the next life to this life, and with that shift has come a growing preoccupation with transience and death. The loss of life's former eternal background makes us only the more aware of time – and in particular, *our* time – slipping away into oblivion. At this point there's a tendency to assume that the basic facts of life and death are the same for us all and ask the same question *of* us all, so that everyone gets more or less the same view of their own mortality. But that I think is not how it is: on the contrary, both the testimony of literature and my personal experience suggest that different people apprehend – or should we say, 'are gripped by'? – the great questions of finitude, transience, contingency, and ultimately, behind everything else, death, in very different ways.

Not to repeat what I have said (or will be saying) elsewhere, it may for example be that men and women face death in typically different ways. Thus if a woman has borne and raised several children, and has seen them off into independence, she may think that she has *already* played her part in creating and in handing over to the next generation, and so she may be content to become increasingly a spectator of a life from which she is now slowly withdrawing. For a man, however, the view is rather different. He is more likely to think of finishing his job and handing over to the next generation much later on, at the time when he makes his will and plans the disposition of his responsibilities and his property. Thus if we think of death first as the big handover, for a woman it is her whole life, all along; whereas for a man it is something he gets round to organizing near the end of his life when he 'puts his affairs in order'. If she believes in life after death, a woman's first question is pretty sure to be: 'Will I see my dear ones again?', whereas a man is much more likely to wonder whether he will be remembered and what his legacy will be.

That is only one of the numerous ways in which the great questions of time and death may present themselves very differently to different people. Thus Heidegger develops a thought that he has picked up from Nietzsche when, in *Being and Time*, he suggests that the sudden realization in middle age of our own mortality functions as an alarm call. I have only a finite time left and therefore must get moving if I am to complete an *opus*, or *œuvre*, or life's work. What the commentators fail to remark is that this is surely a very masculinist view of the meaning of death. For many, many women the transmission of life and of culture to the next generation is their life's chief work. Relatively few women have the ambition to create an enduring *oeuvre*, in the way that so many men strive to do, because for them their enduring *œuvre* is the next generation. Their work is to give life to others and nurture life in others rather than to erect any personal monument.

Another question: if death is a problem, whose death are we talking about? Philip Larkin was obsessively preoccupied with the subject of *his own* death. He thought of death as extinction but hated the thought of being dead, as if after death he might still be hovering about, contemplating his own state of non-existence and perceiving it to be a very cold and lonely condition. But those who accept the young Wittgenstein's arguments to the effect that we cannot ever actually *go through* the process of dying, or experience the state of being dead, Larkin's fears seem to be unfounded. There is nothing in death that I need worry about, or can prepare for. If I have learnt the art of solar living, then I am already living-by-dying all the time, and death's sting is drawn. But I need to acknowledge that although my own death is no problem, there are certain other people who are also mortals, and the death of one of *them* would be a blow from which I could not recover. So my religion frees me from self-concern, but it does not protect me against the general contingency and vulnerability of all life. Nothing can.

These general considerations are enough to indicate how it comes about that different people have very different 'takes' upon the great questions of life, love, work and death, and why I have put forward the view that today, for those of us who have left dogmatic religious belief behind, the religious life nowadays largely takes the form of an attempt to face up to the great questions of life, and to work out one's own personal 'take' on them. Your religion is your personally worked-out and lived philosophy of life and death. At least part of our philosophy of life will consist of saying something like this: at least, no sensible person complains about being a person, and personal life isn't really thinkable at all *except* in a world of finite, temporal Be-ing, in which we are all of us vulnerable to chance and mischance. The best there is for us human beings is to say a wholehearted Yes to the only package deal that is on offer, and try to live life to the full for as long as we have it. That is what ordinary language says nowadays, and we cannot simply disregard it.[7]

On that basis, I build my third and last slogan, which is simply that *solar living is the best religion.* By that I mean that the more we think about the Great Questions and the challenge they present to us, the more we come to understand that there is no way of *escaping* from the basic conditions of life. The only option left is to say Yes to life as a whole and as a package deal: Yes to time, Yes to contingency, Yes to finitude, Yes even to death. Life has no *Telos* – that is, no ultimate Goal – and the practice of solar living attempts to achieve the final happiness by the way one says Yes to life to be spent in the here and now. The effort to live purely affirmatively involves giving up all the *ressentiment*, the complaining, the victim psychology, the censoriousness, the anger, the bitterness, and the festering sense of grievance that poison so many lives, and seem increasingly to poison the whole world of human beings. Instead, we should try to live purely magnanimously and without any negation or discrimination, like the sun.

This purely affirmative, magnanimous living is also *expressive.* One who lives truthfully lives *out*, and *comes* out. Solar ethics rejects ideas of 'inner' reality. It rejects talk of the soul and the inner life, and it rejects any suggestion that we should hold a bit of ourselves back and use it to refer all the time to a Higher World. No, the only 'real' self is the self that is lived out, acted, presented in our daily living, and solar living must reject all ideas of inwardness and instead go for 100 per cent 'all out' expression.

I've said enough to make it clear that I am now less Buddhist and more Romantic and Expressionist than I was until about 1992. I still find a place for meditation, but only as occasional therapy rather than as the daily bread of life. For me, now, Buddhism does not have a satisfactory view of the proper emotional basis of our living and our selfhood. The daily bread of life is a steady stream of outpouring biological (but also culturally elicited and shaped)

---

7 See my *The New Religion of Life in Everyday Speech*, London: SCM Press, 1999.

feeling. This feeling pours out, sustains our selfhood, colours up the world, gives value and is (in brief) what people call *the joys of life*, or simply *joy*. The young Wordsworth was as well able as anyone has ever been to articulate it: he called it 'living by the heart', and I call it 'solar living'. I find something of its spirit cropping up in a great variety of teachers: in the original Jesus, in Blake, in Nietzsche, in Kazantzakis, even in someone like Stanley Spencer. It is my own religious response to our troubled, ambiguous times.

12

On the Meaning of Life

During the nineteenth century, the ordinary person and the world of everyday life gradually moved up the agenda for philosophers and for religious thinkers. Hitherto, both philosophers and theologians had usually regarded the world of ordinary language and everyday life as being a realm of vanity or error, and of no intrinsic interest. Their concern was with what they saw as a more real and enduring World-Beyond, an eternal, metaphysical world of necessary truths (said the philosophers) which at every point underlay the apparent world and gave to it such stability and order as we seem to find in it; and an ideal Heavenly World (according to the theologians) which was the blessed abode of God, spirits and the faithful departed. In their different ways, both Platonic philosophers and monks held that life here below should be oriented towards the eternal world, and to preparing ourselves for death, through which we may hope to enter it.

Thus in the mainstream of Western culture philosophers concentrated on the world of pure thought, and theologians concentrated upon God and sacred things. Both parties tended to see the everyday world of ordinary life and ordinary language as being only secondary and preparatory. The elite of thinkers and priests did not wish to concern themselves with merely transient, secular matters: their minds were fixed on higher things. In any case, until the industrial revolution was well advanced the labouring poor lived such desperately harsh and driven lives that they were almost unreachable. Only religion could help them, by offering them beautiful images of Rest hereafter.

Then during the nineteenth century, a whole series of developments gradually brought the common person and the world of everyday life to the forefront. One may cite, for example, the discovery and collection of folk tales, ballads, fairy tales, folklore and other evidences that there really was such a thing as the *culture* of the common people; the rise to literary prominence of the novel and, with it, of the world of women; the rise of socialism and of liberal democratic politics, bringing with it the view that great historical changes are brought about, not just by the deeds of Great Men, but rather by the struggles and sufferings of the masses; and finally the enhistorization of thought itself, which gradually led us to drop the idea of the thinker as a sort of monk who steps outside history in order to contemplate eternal verities, and instead led us to see all thinking about religion, philosophy and ethics – *and also all the products of such thinking* – as historically conditioned and human.

Through these and other developments, one might say, thought itself during the nineteenth century became steadily more 'enhistorized', more conscious of time and of historical development, and more democratic. Two great figures of the later nineteenth century, Van Gogh and Tolstoy, illustrate the change. A number of the Paris school artists, including Courbet and Pissarro, were socialists and celebrators of the life of ordinary people, but Van Gogh had also an intensely religious temperament that makes his art an extraordinarily 'solar' and ardent affirmation of ordinariness. As for Tolstoy, his moralism and his turn to peasant life had a very great influence upon twentieth-century figures as diverse as Gandhi and Wittgenstein.

Mention of the name of Wittgenstein reminds us of how in the twentieth century the developments I am describing were taken further. People began to think that ordinary language and its world view are always presupposed, and are therefore basic for all of us, so that nobody can pretend to have stepped quite clear of them. Wittgenstein's later writing sees the exploration of ordinariness as being almost the whole task of philosophy. Like the analytical philosophers, he holds that all our thinking is transacted in language, so that the only reliable and objective way to study thought is by studying the way language works; and he also thinks the only way to study ordinary life is by examining the language games and the idioms in which we carry on the business of everyday life. Thus for Wittgenstein the philosophy of ordinary language becomes almost the whole of philosophy. He liked to compare a language with a great city. The ancient, narrow and congested streets in the heart of the old city correspond to ordinary language, compressed, idiomatic and irregular as it is. Around the old city centre the various sciences and branches of knowledge have in modern times grown up like large suburbs, clean and new-built, with broad straight thoroughfares. But the old city centre doesn't go into decline. Its attraction remains. Economically and politically, it still holds the entire city together, and in any case the city lacks major ring roads. All the arterial roads still radiate from the historic centre, so that in order to get from anywhere to any-where else you have to go via the centre. And so people continue to visit the old centre every day: and it continues to be spoken of as being *itself* 'the City'. Notice, too, how the heart of the old City is always a crowded place of *exchange*.

So ordinary language remains basic to the whole of culture. It has its own world view built into it, and when scientists put their theories to the test they don't test them absolutely, but only against the world view, the language and the faculties of sight and hearing that we have to take for granted in the laboratory just as much as we take them for granted in everyday life. High-level dis-course and theorizing, whether in science or religion or philoso-phy or art, still always presupposes ordinariness. For example, I may ask myself 'Am I right in believing that my sense experience gives me evidence of a three-dimensional physical world about me?' Can I *test* the belief in a 3D world about me? No: I can't do experiments at all without *already presupposing* the answer Yes. Thus high-powered science cannot test, but must assume, much of ordinary language and our commonsense world view. It is within the realm of ordinariness that language, world view and the forms of everyday human life and selfhood are first constituted, and we can never leave ordinariness entirely behind. Even where scientific theory corrects our ordinary assumptions, it needs to explain why and within what limits it does so. In the past – Wittgenstein goes on – metaphysical philosophy and supernatural religious belief attempted to soar completely beyond this world and conduct us to a blessed eternal world-above. Now we see that such ambitions were vain: our language gives us only one world, and it is this world; and it fits us for only one life, which is this present life that we are now living. So the last truth in religion becomes clear to us when we recognize the folly of dreams of transcendence and are content to return into and accept the wisdom of ordinary life. The message is very like that of *Mansfield Park* and *Middlemarch*: we need to give up impossible dreams, accept limitation, and learn to be 'faithful over a few things', like the good servants in the parable of the talents (Matthew 25.20–23).

Thus Wittgenstein maintained that philosophical and religious thought, after two-and-a-half millennia of trying to soar away into the blue yonder, now come circling back into ordinariness. We must learn a religious acceptance and affirmation of ordinary life, because in the end it is all there is for us: and Wittgenstein recognized that the necessity and the value of this return into ordinariness has always been a theme of the Jewish, the Christian and some other religions. Even Plato teaches that the philosopher who has achieved enlightenment must go back into the cave for the sake of his fellow humans.

This message, however, is often rejected by ordinary people themselves. They very often see life as a puzzle, and they want to know the answer to it. Legend relates that a taxi driver once recognized that his fare was Bertrand Russell. He took the opportunity to put the great man on the spot by asking him: 'Look here! What's it all about? – that's what I want to know. You tell me: What's it all about?' Legend continues that Russell did not reply, not (presumably) because he couldn't, but because he thought the question was too vague and ill-framed. The taxi driver didn't have a clear idea either of what he was asking, or of what form an answer could take. Similarly, Wittgenstein would have said that if we clearly understand what is happening in the various language games that we play in everyday life, we know all there is to know about what our life is; and apart from that nothing remains except a question about our personal commitment which each one of us must answer for herself. And that is that. A student might say to Wittgenstein: 'Look, in a hundred years we'll all be dead and forgotten, and nothing we've said or done will have made the slightest difference. Doesn't that thought drain all the meaning out of life?' But Wittgenstein would refuse to get involved in that sort of discussion, saying in effect: 'Look: the big question for you is what you are going to do with your own life today and tomorrow. That is all you need to worry about.'

In the past, I have broadly agreed with and followed in the tradition of Russell and Wittgenstein. There is nothing ready-made for us that is 'the Meaning of Life'. There is no Meaning-of-Life laid on for us, out there. But in some recent books I have tried to take the question a little further by examining the way we use words like 'life' and 'it all' in ordinary language, and thereby showing that serious religious and philosophical thinking is already going on in the everyday speech of ordinary people. They are already actively transferring religious attention from the heavenly world to the world of 'life'.

Now I want to take the whole matter a stage further. Bertrand Russell's taxi driver deserves to be taken a bit more seriously than either Russell himself or Wittgenstein would agree to take him, for it is true that in the modern period the question about 'the meaning of life' has become the first question in popular philosophy, and there are good and important reasons why it is such a difficult question to get a hold of and to answer satisfactorily. (I should add, by the way, that in my view 'popular philosophy' fills the place once occupied by metaphysics, and is very important.)

Let us begin by defining 'life' – not an easy matter. We are not here talking about biological life. We are talking of human life, which is social and uniquely highly communicative. Life is the going-on of the process of human existence from birth to death, as it is experienced by a participant in it. One of us. For each of us, 'life' is what is nearest to us, our immediate milieu or field of action. It seems to carry us like a river. I have my life to live, you have yours, and we are both involved in the common life of various groups.

Why then, is life so oddly difficult to get a hold of, and to describe and appraise clearly? The first reason is that 'life' resembles 'consciousness' in that it is always presupposed. We are always involved with it, always already in it, and cannot step outside it in order to get a clear and objective view of it. Life and consciousness are perhaps, both of them, too close to us to be easily seen by us. In recent years there has been a great deal of interdisciplinary interest among scientists and technologists in the problem of consciousness. What is it? Under what conditions does it arise? How can we be sure of detecting its presence, in a machine perhaps, or in an animal? Orthodox scientific method would seem to require us to set up parallel situations which are alike except that in one of them the mysterious property of being conscious is present, and in the other it is excluded. Then we study the differences in behaviour of the two systems under various conditions. But how are we going to do all that *with consciousness*, and what are we to make of the fact that the scientific experimenter cannot set aside *his own* consciousness? It is always present: no science of any kind was ever done or will ever be done except by someone who is himself conscious, and 'in' whose consciousness of it everything happens. Surely the observer's own consciousness is bound to contaminate the experimental situation? And doesn't that show that the problem of consciousness is not a question for science at all, but a question for philosophy?

Consciousness is always there: that no doubt is what is meant by the claim of Descartes that the soul always thinks and (like God) never sleeps. And similarly, life is always there. The world has only ever been described and theorized by us living beings, in life, with an interest in life, and seeing everything from the point of view of life. We don't know of any point of view *except* that of life. A point of view is always not only an *angle*, but also an *interest* that needs to be declared. Only *for life*, for living beings, has there ever actually been a world at all. A living being, and especially a *conscious*, language-using living being, really *needs* to have a world around it, with which it is in exchange, whereas an inanimate being does not have quite the same *need* for a world. So, like consciousness, life is always presupposed and in a sense it embraces everything. The primary world is not any longer the Cosmos, as it used to be: no, the primary world is now the life-world. It is only by life and for the sake of life that a world first gets posited. Life is, one may say, like God in being ubiquitous. It is always present, always the medium in and through which we relate to everything. Life is an ever-running fountain of biological feelings which support a constant hum of symbolic exchange: it is a living being's passionate attachment to, and love and enjoyment of life. That is queer. It is theological, paradoxical: life is . . . the love of life. What do we love when we love life? We love, and are part of, life's own endless, ungrounded, outpouring self-affirmation. It cannot be fully justified or explained: it just *is*. It pours out, and around itself establishes its *habitat*, its world, its *scene*.

We used to believe that God had created for us a ready-made, finished and beautiful Cosmos, and that he had then placed us in it. Innocent and wide-eyed, we took in everything that was presented to us just as it was, finished and ready-made. This was the 'realism' that was appropriate to an epoch when thought was heterological: that is to say, in our thinking we didn't start within ourselves and work outwards through things close to hand, and then on to things farther away: no, in those days thought was typically heterological. It was thinking via Another, and top-down. Things were thought *via* God, and as having come down to us ready-made from God. Thought leapt out, to God and the supernatural world, and from there worked back, and down, to the self. Furthermore, things were characterized in terms of the ways in which they differed from and fell short of the greater Reality from which they had come to us and through which we thought them. Thus, we might try to think our life by comparing it with God's, and say that God's life is eternal, whereas ours is merely *temporal*, God's being is infinite whereas ours is merely *finite*, everything in God is necessary whereas in our life-world everything is *contingent*, and that God's thought of everything including himself is intuitive (simple, immediate, total and simultaneous) whereas our thinking and our processes of exchange are always *discursive*, or language-dependent. In short, our whole tradition was very strongly 'realistic', or heterological. The basic features

of the human condition were thought of as having been anteced-
ently established by God the Creator, who fitted us for them, and
fitted us into them. Thus, if we tried to think our life, we thought
it by contrasting it with the greater life of God – which makes
everything about it seem secondary and derivative. Merely temporal, not eternal; merely contingent, not necessary – and so on.
But, as I have been arguing, in the last two centuries since about
the time of Kant and Hegel we have increasingly struggled to set
aside the old heterological way of thinking, and instead simply
build our world out from ourselves. We are trying to replace the
old metaphysical and theological thinking with a new life-centred
kind of thinking.

When we do this we have to recall that we are not omnipotent
beings who can finish a complete cosmos, bright and beautiful,
all at once. Our human world-building is co-operative, language-
mediated, and extended over time. It is never completed, never
wholly successful and always under review. It is a matter of everyday experience that different individuals have slightly different standpoints, linguistic usages, values and understandings and
will therefore tend to generate conflicting versions of the world.
A paradox thus arises that shows us something about life. When
you and I speak together, we have to be 'transcendental realists',
or we'd never reach any common understanding. By that phrase
I mean that we have to assume that, despite our differences of
'perception', when we communicate with each other, we have to
take what we say as referring to a common objective world that is
the same for both of us. But our differences of standpoint, interests, values and interpretation remain, and ensure that we are still
tending to generate two different worlds, yours and mine, around
ourselves. Real and deep differences of interpretation persist, and
cannot be resolved by appeal to any common facts. So we are
stuck with a combination of 'transcendental realism' with 'empirical relativism', and the paradox here perhaps reflects something about life, namely that it is both one and many, and both
competitive and co-operative. That's the way it is, and the way
we are: insofar as life is competitive, each living thing can't help
but project out its own distinctive version of the world regardless

of what its neighbours say; and insofar as life is co-operative, it is one in us all and rejoices to recognize itself in all its diverse manifestations. It seems that both life's unity and its drive to maximal diversification are fundamental to it.

I have been discussing the difficulty we all find in grasping just what this strange new non-objective thing that we call 'life' is. We used to think of ourselves as coming naked into the world, and finding at once that we are confronted with a complete ready-made scheme of things, a Cosmos into which we fit. Our thinking was strongly heterological. We started with God, we started with the great ready-made Given that presented itself to us, and we worked downwards towards ourselves, understanding ourselves *via* God, and via the cosmic order and the moral order into which we must slot ourselves. Thus, the first form of human self-consciousness was the consciousness of oneself as a sinner before God. Similarly, the ethical question was at first not 'How shall I live?', but 'What is God's will for me?'; and the first form of science was an attempt to grasp a divine order, established *for us*, in the way world-events go. Science began realistic, and of course in many ways still tries to maintain a realist view of the knowledge it generates.

Today, as a result of a long and complicated history, we have come to a more autological kind of thinking. This does not mean that we simply put ourselves in the place of God, for it is obvious that our world picture and our morality are historically evolved products of a debate that still continues. We do not create *ex nihilo*, as God was supposed to do. We need to remember that in our world-building activity we are always subject to certain conditions, which the philosophers have specified in various ways. Remember that we are always within the sphere of Mind (or consciousness or culture: *Geist*), said Idealist philosophy. Remember that you are always a concrete existing individual with an interest in existence, said Kierkegaard. Remember that we are always within language (or the symbolic order), said a whole range of more recent writers, including Wittgenstein, the later Heidegger, and Lacan. I am suggesting (as I have suggested elsewhere), that ordinary people and ordinary language *have already decided* that the best way to appropriate what all these great figures were saying is to use the word 'life'. Remember that life comes first; remember that we are always living beings, in life, and with an intense *interest* in life. It is that *interest* in life that gets us projecting out and differentiating a life-world around ourselves. Remember, too, that life at large precedes one's own individual life, and is much bigger than it is, so that as we have become more aware of life, we have already been given a religious sense of being a part of something much bigger than ourselves.

Seek life first, says D. H. Lawrence. *Life is God*, says Tolstoy. I guess that these two great writers were implicitly attacking the classical view that what we humans most deeply desire and need is what we find in God, namely timelessness, solitude, contemplation and self-sufficiency. On the contrary, we are living beings, and our business is with time, company, action and exchange. The history of Western or Latin Christianity was long dominated by the belief that the best form of Christian life was the life of the contemplative monk or nun, who sought to echo God's eternal, silent, and solitary communion with himself. But if it is true that we are always in life and that life comes first, then we should not follow ascetical practices that attempt to deny our own biology and our own intense communicativeness. We should do the opposite, identifying ourselves wholeheartedly with life's outpouring self-affirmation and its creativity, in ourselves and in others.

In short, my whole argument has suggested that in our post-metaphysical age we no longer have a ready-made Cosmos or a metaphysical God in the quite old way. Instead, we find that the primary reality for us is just life. Indeed, a descriptive account of what ordinary life is and how it works can largely take the place of metaphysics as the basic framework around which we see everything else as being built, and in addition the idioms in ordinary language show that we have already transferred to life much or most of what we used to say about God. It appears that, in the West at least, the old other-worldly religion of deferral has come to fulfilment in a purely this-worldly religion of life.

Here are two brief indications of the change: in the last decade or two, in the principal English-speaking countries, the old funeral service has come to be redescribed as 'A Thanksgiving for the Life of A .B.', and the subsequent memorial service is correspondingly billed as 'A Celebration of the Life of A. B.'. A second indication of the change is the terrorist organizer Osama bin Laden's boast that his people love death as much as we in the West love life. We can cheerfully accept the charge. In the old religious outlook, Death was the first of the Four Last Things and was very close to God. Thus, old people may be described as 'waiting for God' – that is waiting for death. But in the modern West we increasingly associate Life with God, and I think this is a thoroughly healthy development.

It is a development which can in its own way make some appeal to tradition, because in Christian language all three persons of the Trinity are closely associated with life. Thus the God of Israel is surprisingly often simply equated with life – for example in Deuteronomy 30.20 'cleave to him, for he is thy life and the length of thy days'. We are so habituated to imposing a Platonic philosophy on the Old Testament that we have forgotten how straightforwardly naturalistic it often is. It simply does not bother to distinguish between biological vitalism and the more 'orthodox' theological sort of vitalism which calls the Holy Spirit 'the Lord and Giver of life', in the Nicene Creed. Finally, one may add that the Johannine Christ twice identifies himself with life: 'I am the Way, the Truth and the Life', and 'I am the Resurrection and the Life'. And that should be enough to suggest that much of our received religious language can very easily be turned in the direction of a purely this-worldly religion of life, if we wish.

13

What's Happening to Religion?

Asked recently why in his country the ruling family have done so little to modernize political and social life, a member of the Saudi Arabian royal house said simply: 'You see, for us modernization means westernization.' He didn't need to say more: hearing the word 'westernization', people in the Middle East would think instantly of huge Mercedes cars and of the flashy high-rise tourist resorts to be found here and there around the coasts of the Persian Gulf, the Red Sea and the Eastern Mediterranean. To many Arabs, westernization means the almost-unstoppable coming of a world in which everything they have stood for and lived by has simply vanished. It means a wipe-out of Islamic society, culture, religion and morality. It means glittering prosperity in a spiritual desert, and the total disappearance of religion from the world.

The Saudi prince was suggesting that the reason why he can't modernize his country is that Islam and the modern West are so radically opposed to each other that there cannot be any negotiation between them. Liberal, partly modernized religion is impossible. What we see in today's Saudi Arabia is therefore ultra-conservative and totally unmodernized Islam awkwardly coexisting with bits of the gaudy, lurid, fast-approaching modern West. The two worlds try to ignore each other, but such a country can scarcely avoid feeling a sense of acute strain.

In the first decades after the Second World War there had seemed to be more of a choice of possible futures. A developing country had the option of looking, not just to the USA, but also to the socialist bloc, or to the 'non-aligned' group of countries then led by India. The American model wasn't the only game in town.

But since 1990 or so, it has seemed that nothing can now resist the roaring advance of American-style development, as it is currently being experienced in South and East Asia: a populist culture of entertainment and advertising, cheap transport and communications, science-based industrial capitalism and so on. Most Asians seem to be greedy for it, and want to have it all as quickly as possible, even though it means their complete 'detraditionalization' – and they are going to get it. Very soon, little will remain of the old religions except their chief monuments repackaged as tourist attractions, and a few of their customs preserved as picturesque folkways.

The word 'fundamentalism' has many uses nowadays, but one of the best ways to understand it is to see it as a largely lay and populist religious protest against the new order, which takes rather different forms in different faith traditions. Thus nineteenth-century Jews felt threatened by Enlightenment culture, by liberalism, and by their own progressive emancipation. If they were to resist assimilation and to survive as a distinct people, it seemed that the Jews must assert their own difference, go back to Orthodox tradition, and seek a homeland of their own. But among Western Christians the story is rather different, because since late antiquity Christians have seen their own lives against the background of a large-scale cosmological and narrative history of salvation and a supernaturalist view of the world. Nineteenth-century Christians therefore rebelled against all the new ideas that they saw as undermining the authority of Saint Augustine's Grand Narrative of creation, fall and redemption: ideas that include the awareness of deep secular historical change and development, biblical criticism, moral relativism, and in science the naturalistic thinking that eliminates the supernatural and makes humanity just a transient product of Nature.

Thus the form that fundamentalism takes in each major religion is different, as each tradition feels squeezed by modernity in a different way. After almost a thousand years of easy confidence in their own all-round superiority to Christians and in the finality of their own faith, Muslims have been very hard-hit by the decline of the Ottoman Empire and the political humiliations they have suffered in the past two centuries. It is not altogether surprising that their religious reaction should take the form of a political fight-back against the West, for it must seem to them that all their troubles and the threats they face come precisely from the West's continuing cultural and economic domination of their part of the world.

Each tradition, I am suggesting, tries to find its own way of fighting back against the forces that threaten to dissolve it. The resulting so-called 'fundamentalisms' may seem to us to be very naïve, populist and anti-theoretical; but we should not underestimate them, for they sometimes enter into surprisingly successful alliance with the forces of rapid development. Thus in India's recent general election the BJP, the 'Hindu fundamentalist' party not only claimed to be the best defender of traditional Hindu faith and values, but also tried to take the credit for India's current economic boom. Similarly, in Texas and elsewhere Evangelical Christian 'fundamentalism' today readily enters into alliance with the most rip-roaring predatory capitalism. Hence the strange paradox, so disconcerting to old-fashioned religious liberals, of a union between the most aggressively self-righteous, powerful and wealthy forces in society and neo-conservative religion. It is common: we see it equally in the piety of the princes of the house of Saud, in the Evangelicalism of Texan oil millionaires and in the devotion of Indian property speculators. We liberals thought that *we* were the more up-to-date ones, and that *they* were a bit backward. But the 'neo-con' phenomenon suggests that the boot is on the other foot. Because religious conservatives always take a very pessimistic view of secular society and of human nature, they are not so shocked as religious liberals are by the harshly competitive face of capitalism – while in return the capitalists are as happy to use religion as they are to use anything else that can be useful to them.

Consider, for example, how the global media magnate Rupert Murdoch is a conservative populist in each and every country where his newspapers and broadcasting stations operate. Everywhere he brandishes the local totems, presses the right local buttons, and uses the local passwords. For a multinational company it's just good practice to ally oneself with the local gut-politics – both the local form of nationalism, and the local brand of nostalgic conservative religion. For their part, the old-time believers are only too happy to be befriended: they feel that to be befriended by the powerful is a kind of validation, and they seem not to be troubled by the thought that they may be selling their own souls.

Against this background, we can understand the three most-conspicuous forms that are taken by religion today.

There is, first, religion as *heritage*, preserved as a tourist attraction, mummified, unalterable in even the smallest particular, and (of course) quite dead. Society preserves it very determinedly, not just because it brings in tourist money, but also because it includes so many important tokens of continuing cultural 'identity'. Visiting Scandinavia recently, I was struck by the immaculate 'presentation' of the principal Lutheran parish churches. Most people don't *personally* practise or believe in Christianity any more, but they do know all about their Lutheran state Church, and they preserve the shell of it jealously, because for so long as it is still there the national tradition seems to remain intact. All's well: nothing has changed.

Secondly, there is so-called *fundamentalist* religion, right-wing, fiercely anti-intellectual, militant, and highly ethnocentric in outlook. This kind of religion is by no means an empty shell. On the contrary, it really *is* believed and practised. It binds people closely together in using their own internally intelligible vocabulary as a system of passwords, in being extremely self-righteous, and in hating outsiders. It is usually a strange amalgam of zealous popular religiosity and militant nationalism. It produces no literature of merit, and its leadership is of the 'charismatic' type. Often it is financially supported by rich people on the political Right.

Thirdly, there is what remains of *liberal* religion, as it survives among some Christians, Jews, Buddhists, and perhaps a few other faith traditions. This is religion that does have an ancient philosophical tradition, that attempts to be rational, and that purports to have come to terms with modern critical ways of thinking. It still occupies most of the traditional seats of religious authority in the great temples, universities, and monasteries, and it reckons to have made peace with the modern world. But the sad truth is that it is nowhere near as rational as it thinks it is. It has failed badly, and is now in headlong decline.

Such are the three most conspicuous kinds of religion that survive today; and they are all horrible. Nowhere is religion in a healthy and settled relationship with modernity. Heritage religion is dead, liberal religion is weak and fading fast, and fundamentalist religion is irrational and morally detestable. Frankly, I can't stand any of them, and it is against this unhappy background that I have over the years so often asked what religion can be for us today, and have tried to reinvent it. How am I to find a form of religion that I personally can follow without constantly feeling acutely embarrassed and uncomfortable?

As you will already have observed, I am thinking that Nigel Leaves is right to suggest that one of the most constant themes of all my thinking and writing has been the critique of religion. And the main starting point has been an idea I had in 1979, when (as I remember) I was telling people that I was trying to take up Kant's old arguments for the autonomy of ethics, and apply them to religion.

The main issues here are pretty straightforward. Until early modern times most human beings had always felt most at ease with a mythical style of thinking that somehow manages to tell us how everything began and came into its present form, what is the supreme Power, whom we should obey and worship, and by what law we should live – all in one story. Religion included basic cosmology, science, political theory, theology and ethics, all interwoven with each other. But after Galileo and Descartes – one might say, during the 1660s – people began to recognize that the new mathematical physics gives us a science of nature that is theologically and morally quite neutral. The world was pictured as a machine, and in terms of matter, motion and number *only*. All talk of values and purposes was left out.

The long-term result of this was to be a growing crisis in moral philosophy and in religious thought. Instead of the old, loose, grand unity in which society's founding religious myths somehow held everything together, culture was breaking up into a number of distinct, autonomous subjects – of which of course mathematical physics was the first and most prestigious. You could no longer read purposes or values, or indeed the Hand of God, directly off the way the world machine works. Even as late as the 1680s, a book like Sir Robert Filmer's *Patriarcha* (published posthumously in 1680, and several times reprinted) still traced all social and political authority back to a religious foundation – to Genesis, to the rule of Adam over Eve and of God over everything. But in the new world of modernity you cannot expect God to underpin everything in quite that way. The new world is a world of distinct subjects, each of which needs to work out its own justification. In ethics, for example, you need to show that morality is reason in practice, and that we act morally when we act on principles that we ourselves have seen to be rational and have freely taken upon ourselves.

It is in this context that Kant introduces his phrase 'the autonomy of ethics', and I can now try to explain the idea. In our childhood morality was at first taught to us with the backing of sanctions. We were rewarded for keeping the rules, and punished for breaking them. In effect, this early morality was imposed and enforced by Authority: it was a matter of law and prudence. But as we grew up we gradually began to see the point of morality, and to internalize its demands. The sanctions become less important, and eventually fall away, as we learn that the basic principles of morality deserved to be adopted and followed by us just for their own sakes. The sanctions are redundant. And when we understand that morality doesn't need any external justification – in fact, is better without it – then our own morality has become autonomous; whereas morality imposed by an external authority and backed by sanctions is 'heteronomous'.

So there it is: in our childhood morality was at first imposed upon us by parental authority, and it was prudent to do as you were told. But we only reach moral maturity when our morality has become fully our own, and we freely choose to do the right thing just because it is right. No external authority is needed either to lay the Law down, or to enforce it. True morality is moral living that has become fully autonomous, rational, and freely chosen.

In politics the same arguments lead to liberal democracy: free people are people who choose their own government and its policies. That is 'freedom under the law'. *We* made the law and gave it its authority over us.

Now, my suggestion in 1979 was that I would use similar arguments to try to establish 'the autonomy of religion'. Our usual ideas about true religion are highly heteronomous: religion is the worship of a God who is all-powerful and all-knowing, who has himself revealed all the principles of true religion to us, including the Creed, the path to salvation, ethics and right worship. If we follow the ways of true religion God will give us a heavenly reward, but if we rebel against God and stray from the right path then God will sentence us to eternal punishment in Hell. Thus God has graciously given us the true religion to live by, and the strongest-possible incentives for following it. Clear enough, but if we apply to this case the arguments for ethical autonomy we are bound to conclude that our practice of religion is purer and more disinterested if it is *not* driven by the hope of Heaven and the fear of Hell. More than that, I quickly concluded that if we are ever to reach a fully mature and autonomous spirituality, our practice of religion must become independent of any external justification or enforcement. And that means giving up all realist ideas of God, of religious truth, and of what we are doing in prayer and worship.

I was thus coming to the view that religious attitudes, beliefs and practices could be, and should be, adopted, cultivated, and pursued just for their own sakes, as intrinsically good, and good for us. The religious life was simply the good life. As such it need not depend upon belief in doctrines about a very powerful person who imposes true religion upon us with terrifying threats: it may simply be *chosen*. But what sort of personal qualities are involved here? Back in 1979/1980 I was still very much an admirer of Kant, Hegel and Kierkegaard, and in addition because I was a thinker by profession I was highly conscious of what a hard spiritual struggle it is to get one's own ideas straight. This made me long for spiritual freedom, and not least freedom from the self-regard and the narrow focus of the biological drives. I admired selflessness, expansiveness, lightness (or levity), clarity of consciousness, and easy mastery, In a word, *Eckhart*. I tended to associate religion with spiritual and imaginative largeness and liberality, and with intensified consciousness.

All these ideas went into a book which I titled *The Autonomy of Religion*, and duly sent in to my publisher in early 1980. He was tickled by the seemingly novel argument that in order to purify religion and make it free we must get rid of the notion of God's objective, personal reality. He thought the book could be a big seller, and that it might help to bring back something of the excitement that had been stirred up by *Honest to God* some 15 or 20 years earlier. But it needed a more seductive title. So he looked at the quotation from Eckhart that I'd put on the title page, and retitled the book *Taking Leave of God*. Then he talked me into agreeing with his proposal.

The book duly appeared in the autumn of 1980, caused a fuss, and has remained in print more-or-less continuously. Unfortunately, however, the re-titling fatally obscured its main message, and to this day even professional philosophers of religion – including some people who have published books about Kant – continue absurdly to misrepresent the book's main argument. But there it is. The liveliness of the controversy stimulated me to begin an intellectual journey and literary project which still goes on, and I see now that all the way along I have been struggling to get clear about and to articulate one question above all: What can religion be for us today?

My journey has taken me away from Kierkegaard. His spirituality involved the cultivation of a second, hidden, interior life of subjectivity, or 'hidden inwardness'. It involved a heightened subjective consciousness. One's religious life was one's *inner* life. That I now reject vehemently, and my spirituality has instead become a spirituality of 'coming out' and free self-expression that I call 'solar living'. I reject Kierkegaard's Platonism, which leads him to lay great emphasis on the old binary contrast between outer appearance and inner reality. Instead, I see the world and our life as nothing but a solar process of pouring out and passing away – a process into which we should simply cast ourselves. For I also reject the old, platonic, opposition between the timeless and eternally real Being of God, and the transient Becoming of creatures. For me, all being is temporal 'be-ing'. In the past, God was actually defined as Being-Itself; so I now translate commitment to God into commitment to Being, which is commitment to Be-ing, which is our human existence, which is life, which is our continual self-expression and communication with others. Thus I now translate the old commitment to God's eternal, transcendent Being into an immediate commitment to our own be-ing, our own life in the here and now. At the same time, I have also come to reject Plato's 'supernaturalism of reason', and I now take a much more emotivist view of the self. I see the life of the self as consisting of a continuous outpouring flow of feeling. When it is strong enough, this outpouring feeling (which is always a feeling for life, *Lebensgefühl*) can break free of its usual biological reference and focus, and become selfless and universal. True religion then is solar living, which is a whole-hearted commitment to life, which is based on universal love for the world, for life, and for all living things. And eternal happiness is an outpouring joy in life that we can learn and that will never wholly forsake us, however bad things may get to be.

There is thus a wide gap between my religious values of 25 years ago – the time when I was writing *Taking Leave of God* (1980) – and today. Back in 1979/80 I was still much influenced by Plato and the older Western Christian spirituality. I admired Meister Eckhart, Kant, Hegel, and Kierkegaard, and I saw the religious life in rather masculine terms. One should aim for a heightened subjective consciousness, free, light-footed, and emancipated from Nature.

Today – and especially since the upheaval of the early 1990s – my outlook has changed greatly. I have rejected Plato's classic binary oppositions, and now regard all Be-ing as contingent, finite, and temporal. The world-process is a fountain of contingencies that continually pours out and passes away, and we are simply parts of it. Accordingly, I have abandoned the old spirituality of hidden inwardness, and replaced it by a spirituality of life, seen as a continual 'coming out' into expression. We should accept and affirm our own unity with the pouring-out and passing-away of everything, of which we are part. We should learn to say a wholehearted Amen to our own lives. We should find eternal joy in the present moment, in our own continual passing away. We should burn with love for the world, for life and for each other. We should simply abandon all traditional ideas about what used to be called 'the left hand of God' – ideas about sin, wrongdoing, guilt, judgement, reprobation, punishment, Hell, and so forth – and try to be as comprehensively affirmative as we possibly can.

And so on – in brief, I no longer seek salvation either by escaping from this world like the orthodox, or by transcending it in thought like my own earlier self. I want simply to affirm and to love our transient and contingent life in the here and now. I have invented and quoted various terms for the trick that I am trying to describe here, and you may recognize some of them: 'ecstatic naturalism', 'solar living', 'ecstatic immanence', 'glory', 'natural supernaturalism', 'the mysticism of secondariness', 'entostasy', and so on. None of these expressions has, as yet, quite caught on, but the idea is as old as the Gospels, and it crops up repeatedly in modern literature. It is that in order to find religious truth, we don't need to seek an entirely different world of invisible and timeless things. No, we should find it in the transient, contingent world of the here and now. The mote dancing in the sunbeam, shadows, flames, bubbles, a transient expression flickering across a face, saxifrages, the wings of insects, a summer's evening, Our rapture should be a purely immanent delight in all this, just here, now.

Now you may ask: If religion is to become entirely a matter of the way we give ourselves into life in the here and now, what room is there for any kind of religious apparatus of the kind we've known hitherto? Surely, what I've been describing is a kind of mysticism – something that will always appeal to a few poets, nature lovers, and photographers maybe . . . but certainly *not* something that could ever function as a complete working religion and become established as part of the lives of most ordinary people?

I reply that, in the traditional language of Christianity, what I am describing is the immediate, 'kingdom' type of religion that has since biblical times been expected one day to replace the mediated, 'ecclesiastical' type of religion that we are all accustomed to.

Historically, Christianity has mostly been ecclesiastical. It was assumed that times were very hard, that a strict social discipline was needed, and that people must be taught that the supreme religious happiness they yearn for is still a long way ahead – either in the far future, or (for most of us) after our deaths. Meanwhile, in the present blighted state of the everyday human world, we can make our lives bearable and give them the right direction by constantly cultivating the thought of the blessed, supernatural world above, and by negotiating with it. Religion is therefore *mediated*: it concentrates on the supernatural world, on holy scriptures, on doctrines, on acts of worship, on the veneration of a range of holy figures, and on building up the great institution of the Church, all in order to gain the right direction, the confidence, and the strength for our daily life in the everyday world. Our relation to everydayness is mediated by the supernatural world that one day we hope to see for ourselves. 'Thy Kingdom come,' we say.

That's the kind of religion we are used to: but why has everything changed?

I reply that over a long period in our cultural tradition the focus of religious attention has been gradually shifting from the heavenly world above to this world, from the long-term future to the present, and from a God-centred to a Christ-centred, or simply human-centred, outlook. Our whole view of this life and this present world has been getting much less pessimistic. We no longer have to live under strict social discipline and absolute monarchy: a free society and liberal democracy are now possible. Everybody can in principle enjoy a full span of life, a decent sufficiency, and civil peace. More than that, our whole life-world has become highly aestheticized and we now take it for granted that we can and should **enjoy life** in a way our remoter ancestors could only dream of. The kingdom-type of religion, immediate, and finding eternal happiness in the here and now, is ready to be lived and enjoyed by ordinary people. The great supernatural apparatus of mediated religion is now largely redundant, and we should instead be concentrating upon the new religion of ordinary life.

Am I simply saying that modern Western secular culture is the Kingdom of God on earth? No, I am not. On the contrary, I insist that modern Western people are still largely stuck in the ecclesiastical period and its mediated living. Instead of pouring ourselves out into the living of our own lives, we still waste too much of our time dreamily living vicarious lives with the help of dramas acted out on cinema and television screens. Instead of becoming gods and saints ourselves, we venerate celebrities, copy their fashions and parrot their opinions. We are still a long way short of entering upon our full inheritance – which leaves something for religion to do in the future. As always, religion should battle to persuade people that we and our world are still a lot less than we can and should be. Puritans and Evangelicals often darkly suspect that ordinary people are enjoying life too much: I'm dissatisfied for the opposite reason. I say that we are not yet enjoying life nearly enough.

14

The Religion of Ordinary Life

Almost all of religion hitherto has been based on a clear distinction between two great realms, the profane world of everyday, secular human life and the sacred world. Various bits of the everyday world were designated 'holy' because they mediated contact or interaction between the two worlds. Thus there were a holy land, a holy people, a sacred language, sacred writings, holy places, buildings, rituals and so on. It was somehow desperately important to secure the favour and the blessing of the spirits and gods, and the various appointed channels through which you could access divine presence, forgiveness, and grace were very highly regarded.

The question arises, why was secular life somehow unendurable or impossible without supernatural favour? Why was the mighty apparatus of religious mediation so important? Briefly, it appears that human beings were very anxious and very needy. Our ignorance, our sense of the precariousness of life, and the certainty of death were so overwhelming that almost no human being could contemplate, head-on and calmly, the facts of the human condition, and then go on to live a contented, autonomous secular life. Human beings simply could not bear to live without very elaborate protective fictions and the whole apparatus of mediated religion.

In modern times – and especially since about 1850 – everything has changed. The sacred world of religion and the everyday human life-world have merged and have become identical. It feels like the end of history, in rather the same way and for much the same reasons as the gradual decay of monarchy and caste or class society; and the emergence of liberal democracy as the last form of political organization, also feels (to some, at least) like the end of history. Indeed, you may say that in both cases what's happened is that certain great disciplinary institutions that used to be thought of as 'absolutes', and as permanently necessary to human well-being, have now come to the end of their useful life. We don't need them any more: we can manage on our own.

In the case of religion, I am suggesting that the end of religion as we have so far known it comes when people no longer need to be governed by religious law, nor to be supported by stories and beliefs about supernatural beings. Religion instead becomes immediate: it's now about your attitude to your own life, and the way you see it as fitting into the larger stream of human life in general. It is about the way you negotiate your own deal with life and its basic conditions: its temporality, its precariousness, your freedom, and your coming death. It is about how we can find eternal joy just in the mere living of our ordinary lives. We no longer 'look up' in any way at all: we've learnt the trick of living so intensely that we do not expect ever again to be seriously troubled by the old fears.

This event is forecast in the Bible, for example in the prophet Jeremiah's promise of a new covenant and in the account of the Day of Pentecost in the Acts of the Apostles, and also by the long tradition of talk about the coming of the Kingdom of God on earth. In the later Christian tradition the secular realm begins to assert itself in the late Middle Ages, in seventeenth-century Protestantism in countries like Holland, and above all in the emergence of liberal democracy and the middle-class leadership of industrial society after the French Revolution. After about 1870, with rising prosperity and better sanitation, ordinary urban life is suddenly innocent, and different. But perhaps the most striking recent manifestation of 'the new religion of life' was the height of protest-and-pop youth culture in the late 1960s. Tradition and the authority of the older generation died, and Europe became a whole lot more secular than before. Organized religion has been in galloping decline ever since.

Elsewhere I have argued that one of the best ways to convince sceptics of the reality of the changes I am describing is to study the flood of new idioms about life that have entered the language in the last forty years. It seems undeniable that a great deal of religious attention has now been transferred from God to life. Life itself – as we see in the later writings of the critic F. R. Leavis – has become the religious object. I need to come to terms with life, I need to gain control over my own life, I need to live my own life in my own way, I need to enjoy what people call 'the feeling of being alive', and I need to love life intensely, and live it to its fullest. A kind of heroic, courageous faith in life and a determination to engage with it and make the most of it is the gateway to victory over anxiety and death, and will show us how we can find 'life-satisfaction' in making our own modest contribution to the building (and also the renewal) of the common human life-world.

That's the agenda, in brief. I don't need to write any apologetics for this new universal human religion, because it is now quietly slipping into place all over the world. It needs no help from me, nor from anyone else. But I do want to present its 'systematic theology' as shortly and as clearly as I possibly can, so that people can see a little better what we are losing, and what we are gaining. Here then is a very brief outline, with a few marginal comments. As you read it, remember that my claim is that most or all of this you already know. I'm not pretending to be introducing anything at all odd or unheard-of. What I am presenting is already mostly platitudinous.

Life

1   Life is everything.

Life is the whole human world, everything as it looks to and is experienced by the only beings who actually have a world, namely human beings with a life to live.

2   Life is all there is.

Our age is now post-metaphysical. The world of life is not dependent upon, nor derived from, any other realm, nor is there any other world after it, or beyond it.

3 *Life has no outside.*

Everything is immanent, interconnected, secondary. Everything remains within life. When we are born, we don't come *into* this world, and when we die we don't *leave* it. There is no absolute point of view from which someone can see 'the Truth', the final Truth, about life.

4 *Life is God.*

Life is that in which 'we live and move and have our being' (Acts 17.28), within which we are formed, and of whose past we will remain part. Both our ultimate Origin and our Last End are within life. Life is now as God to us.

5 *To love life is to love God.*

Every bit of our life is final for us, and we should treat all life as a sacred gift and responsibility. We should see our relation to life as being like an immediate relation to God. We are moved and touched by the way all living things, and not just we ourselves, spontaneously love life, affirm it and cling to it.

6 *Life is a continuous streaming process of symbolic expression and exchange.*

The motion of language logically precedes the appearing of a formed and 'definite' world. It is in this sense that it was once said that 'In the beginning was the Word'.

Life and My Life

7 *My life is my own personal stake in life.*

The traditional relation of the soul to God is now experienced in the form of the relation between my life and life in general. As, traditionally, one's first responsibility in religion was for the salvation of one's own soul, so now a human being's first duty is the duty to recognize that I simply am the life I have lived so far, plus the life that still remains to me.

8   *My life is all I have, and all I'll ever have.*

I must *own* my own life, in three senses: I must claim it wholly as mine, acknowledge it, and assume full responsibility for the way I conduct it. I must live my own life in a way that is authentically mine. To be authentically oneself in this way – the opposite of 'living a lie' – is the first part of the contribution each of us should seek to make to life as a whole.

9   *Every human person has, in principle, an equal stake in life.*

This principle is vital to our ideas of justice and of love for the fellow-human being. Murder and other offences against the person are almost everywhere regarded as equally serious, whoever the victim is. The love of God is love and fellow-feeling for 'the neighbour' – or the fellow creature – generalized without limit until it becomes the love of all life.

10   *In human relationships, justice is first in order, but love is first in value.*

We should esteem love most highly of all; but love itself must be based on justice, not least in parental/filial and in sexual relationships. The work of justice is to clear a level space for love.

The Limits of Life

11   *Life is subject to limits. In life, everything is subject to temporality.*

In life everything is held within and is subject to the movement of one-way linear time. Life is, as people say, a single ticket: there are no second chances or retakes.

12   *In life, everything is contingent.*

In life, the one-way linear movement of time makes every moment final and every chance a last chance; but at the same time everything is contingent. This painful combination of finality with contingency is what gives rise to people's talk of luck or fate. More to the point, it also follows that there are no fixed or unchanging absolutes in life. There are no clearly and permanently fixed realities, or identities, or even standards.

13   *Life itself, and everything in the world of life, is*
mediated by language.

Consciousness is an effect of the way language lights up the world of experience, and self-consciousness is an effect of the use of language to talk about itself. Thought is an incompletely executed motion of language somewhere in our heads.

14   *Life goes on, but my life is finite.*

The only deaths we need to prepare ourselves for are the deaths of others who are dear to us. We will never experience our own deaths. So we should simply love life and say Yes to life until our last day. There is no point at all in making any other preparation for death.

Faith in Life

15,   *When I have faith in life, love life, and commit myself*
to it, I have bought a package deal: life with its limits.

Whereas in traditional theology 'evil' was seen as a secondary intruder into an originally perfect world, and therefore as being eliminable, the limits of life, which were traditionally called 'metaphysical evil' or 'evils of imperfection', are essential to life. Unlike God, life is finite and imperfect, and has to be accepted as being neither more nor less than what it is. If I want to refuse the package, the alternative for me is 'passive nihilism' or thoroughgoing pessimism. For the religion of life, apologetics takes the form of an attempt to show that pessimism is unreasonable.

16 *The package deal of life cannot be renegotiated.*

There is nobody to renegotiate the deal with. We cannot hope to vary the terms on which life is offered to us.

17 *Life is bittersweet, and bittersweetness is greatly to be preferred to pure sweetness.*

In the classic iconography of Heaven, everyone is 33 years old, everyone looks the same, and everything is oddly dead, like a plastic flower on a grave. In real life, we love imperfections, irregularities, beauty spots, and signs of frailty or age. The mortal actual is far more loveable than the ideal.

18 *We should never complain, nor even feel any need to complain.*

Life should be loved purely affirmatively and exactly as it is. Everyone gets basically the same deal, and nothing else is on offer. Any sense of victimhood or paranoia or grievance is out of place, and we should get it out of our systems. Never say, nor even *think* 'Why me?'

Solar Living

19 *Life is a gift (with no giver) that is renewed every day, and true religion is expressive, 'solar' living.*

By faith, and without any qualification or restriction, I should let life well up in me and pour itself out into symbolic expression through me. Thus I 'get myself together': we become ourselves by expressing ourselves.

20 *Solarity is creative living-by-dying.*

In solar living I live by dying, because I am passing away all the time. In my symbolic expression I get myself together, but as I do so I must instantly pass on and leave that self behind. I must not be *attached* to my own life, nor to my own products, or expressed selves. My self, and all my loves, must be continuously let go of and continuously renewed. Dying therefore no longer has any terrors for me, because I have made a way of life out of it.

21 *Solar living creates great joy and happiness.*

My symbolic expression may take various forms, as it pours out in my quest for selfhood, in my loves or my work. In all these areas, continuous letting-go and renewal creates joy, which on occasion rises and spills over into cosmic happiness. This 'cosmic' happiness is the modern equivalent of the traditional *summum bonum*, the 'chief end' of life.

22 *Even the Supreme Good must be left behind at once.*

I, all my expressions, and even the *summum bonum*, the Supreme Good itself, are all of them transient. Eternal happiness may be great enough to make one feel that one's whole life has been worthwhile, but it is utterly transient. Let it go!

The End of 'The Real World'

What people call 'reality' is merely an effect of either power, or habit.

23 *The Real: a product of lazy, unthinking habits of perception and interpretation.*

The fixity and unchangeability that people like to ascribe to the real world out there is in fact merely the effect upon them of their own lazy habits. They are in a rut of their own making.

24   *There is no ready-made Reality out there.*

There is no ready-made meaningfulness out there, and no objective Truth out there. Meaning is found only in language, and truth belongs only to true statements. Because life is always language-wrapped, everything in the world of life is always shaped by the language in which we describe it, and in a living language everything is always changing. It follows that we ourselves, and our language, and our world, are shifting all the time like the sea. Nothing is, nor can it be, objectively and permanently fixed.

25   *We ourselves are the only Creator.*

As we become critically aware, the objective world melts away. So many supposed features of the world turn out to be merely features of the language in which we describe it. By now, critical thinking has dissolved away objective reality, leaving us with just the human worldwide web, the stream of all our human activity and conversation, and the changing consensus-world-picture that it generates. Our world is our communal, partly botched work of folk art.

26   *Nihilism and creative freedom.*

There is no stable real world and no enduring real self. But this situation is not one for despair: it offers us the freedom to remake ourselves and our world. By solar living we can each of us make a personal offering, a small contribution to life, an oblation.

Death

27   *Passing out into life.*

Unattached, but loving life to the last, I am able at the end of my life to pass out into the moving flow of life in general. The only sensible preparation for death is the practice of solar living.

* * * * *

In 27 brief theses, I have tried to present a short systematic theology of the religion of life that (I think) most people in the West already believe, or are coming to believe. It is already built into our everyday speech. Some people may prefer to describe it as a philosophy of life (German, *Lebensphilosophie*). Other people may wish to think of it as the final stage of the historical development of religion, to which Christianity itself looks forward, under such slogans as the nineteenth-century phrase 'building the Kingdom of God on earth'. I don't mind: I don't think it matters too much, and I certainly would not wish to privilege either any particular doctrinal formulation or any particular technical terms.

15

The Ethics of Value Creation

In about the year 1960, as a young curate in a South Lancashire parish, I was privileged to witness what may have been one of the last great examples of a public death, 'a good death' in the grand manner.[1] The person in question was a redoubtable old matriarch of the parish, whose entire descent-group of children, grandchildren and great-grandchildren used to assemble for lunch at her house every Sunday. Now in her late eighties, she had taken to her bed and was known to be dying. Her last important act was to summon all her ancient enemies – and they were very numerous – to her bedside and forgive them all unconditionally. It was hardly an occasion on which her enemies could argue back at her. They had no alternative but to accept her generous forgiveness of their supposed sins and slink silently away, eternally one-down. Meanwhile the old lady went off to join the Church Triumphant, eternally one-up on all her foes. They could not retaliate now. She had given checkmate, and the blame game was over. She was the victor; hers was the crown of life. That was how a Christian should die – understanding the logic of the blame game so well as to make quite sure that you die in the odour of sanctity and feeling really good, while at the same time you have ensured that everyone else is left behind feeling really bad, forever indebted to you and morally inferior.

Such is the logic of the traditional ideas of forgiveness and reconciliation. They always involve a power struggle: somebody

---

1 I confess to having used this anecdote before, in Leo Howe and Alan Wain (eds), *Predicting the Future*, Cambridge: Cambridge University Press, 1993, p.169. But it is still true, and very apposite here.

always comes out on top. You may say that religious people are people who are smart enough to know that in the long run it is the *moral* advantage that counts for most, and so are careful to be sure that they always have it. And if the old lady's enemies felt annoyed that she had outmanoeuvred them, then it could always be pointed out to them that they too could play the same trick when their own last days came. And is it not common knowledge that everywhere people *do* in fact battle for the moral high ground, in a way that ensures that the dead are always morally superior to the living, as women are morally superior to men, and as respectable and well-housed people are superior to those who are down and out?

The assumptions behind my example are now becoming clear. Why is it so important to die 'in a state of Grace'? Because the whole of our human life is spent in making preparations for a great court case after we die, at which our eternal destiny will be decided. We've got to ensure that our accounts are fully prepared, ready for audit, and that our reputations are spotless. We cannot afford to have any skeletons in our closets, because the soul at our Last Assize will be in the same sort of position as the defendant in a great libel case. We need to look and to be really fragrant.

But why this conception of human life, and how we should spend it? Because at the time when our religious traditions were taking shape the first legal systems were being graven on stones and codified in books. It was inevitable that thinking about morality should come to be saturated in legal metaphors. The Universe was modelled on the state, and God was its absolute Monarch. He promulgated the laws of physical Nature and also the Moral Law that governs the actions of all rational creatures. Irrational creatures obey the natural law by physical necessitation. Rational creatures are morally necessitated to obey the moral law, and are given consciences to tell them so. In addition, it was widely believed that there is at least a partial enforcement of the moral law by God even during this life, which functions to remind us of the Final Accounting that still lies ahead of us. Prudence pays; honesty is even in purely this-worldly terms already the best policy. Thus the Psalmist declares confidently:

> I have been young, and now am old; yet I have not seen the righteous forsaken or his children begging bread. (Psalm 37.25)

And this claim, that human life is here and now already subject to a Moral Providence that will ultimately (and indeed, *literally*) have the Last Word, could still be made seriously in the eighteenth century by the celebrated Anglican apologist, Bishop Joseph Butler.[2] Which prompts a thought: in litigious countries where the legal system is very well established, people are quick to learn the art of working the system to their own advantage. And where people are similarly sure of a long-established moral and religious system which is modelled on the civil law, it is not altogether surprising that they should learn to operate the religious system to their own advantage, too. Which indeed is just what my beloved old matriarch was doing. She was playing the moral card, and in a situation in which it was her Ace of trumps. She was securing victory for herself in a power game, the power game that completely dominates human life, and not least among the religious.

To take another and much less edifying example, consider the fierce struggle for power that has dominated the life of Anglicans and others in recent decades. The Conservative Evangelicals have been playing a part rather like that of Militant and other near-Trotskyite 'entryists' in the Labour Party. They have been battling to get in and take over, and have done so by ceaselessly claiming sole legitimacy for themselves. As the hard Left claim to be the only real socialists, so the Evangelicals are in the habit of using language designed to get us all into the way of assuming that *they* are the only true Christians, and even the only true *Anglicans*. This is odd, because the Church of England is a rather medieval type of 'broad' folk church, a 'school for sinners', episcopally governed and (since the Reformation) basically Lutheran. There

---

2 Joseph Butler, 1736, *The Analogy of Religion Natural and Revealed to the Constitution and Course of Nature*.

could hardly be a Church *less* suitable for the Evangelicals, with their strange mixture of pop Calvinism and campfire revivalism. They notoriously have no respect at all for the authority of bishops, so why do they so much want to *be* bishops?

In the British situation, the answer is of course that the Evangelicals greatly covet the historic social standing and wealth of the Church of England (or what's left of it), and they are willing to play any card that will give them an advantage in their struggles for power. Homosexuality is currently proving just the right issue for them. In other areas they will play other cards, exploiting popular anxieties about medical research in order to combat the way in which doctors and life scientists are nowadays tending to take over large areas of 'bioethics', and exploiting the gap between the Creeds and the results of biblical criticism in order to defeat liberal theology.

Enough. In religion there is very often a struggle for power between different factions or sects, and we seem always to find the high ground occupied by those who have most successfully appropriated to themselves the language of legitimacy. They are the orthodox, the traditionalists, the real thing: the ones who believe what has always been believed. In Judaism, modernizers have struggled to find a word that will give them some leverage against the Orthodox majority. Different groups have called themselves Liberal, Reformed, Progressive and even 'Conservative' – but to no avail. The Orthodox remain in the saddle. Similarly in Islam the Sunnis always come first, and the Shias and all the other smaller groups will always be second. In Western Christianity the Church's patience has ensured that even in countries that were staunchly anti-Catholic for four centuries Protestantism has been slowly ground down and now comes second to Catholicism again. Morally, at least, Catholicism is back on the high ground, even in Britain and Holland – or so it hopes.

Both within the Churches and in the larger world outside them, what is rather optimistically called 'morality' plays a prominent part in battles for social prestige and authority. Within the Churches, especially in rural areas, the remaining faithful are all too often people whose religion and morality functions to make their armoured self-satisfaction still more impenetrable. Outside the Churches, everyone will have noticed that morality is nearly always preached downwards. Those who are relatively more old, rich and socially secure deliver moral lectures to those who are younger, poorer and less long-resident. The old, rich and powerful not only always assume their own moral superiority; they keep on and on reminding us of it. Moral talk rarely has much effect upon its audience, because its real purpose is to make the *speaker* feel even more self-satisfied. Both in religion and in ethics, people's biggest need is for a strong subjective assurance of moral justification or legitimacy. In religion I want to be really sure that I am one of God's Elect, and in morality I want to be quite sure that *my* morality is the only really *moral* morality; that I really am *better* than my neighbour. That's the function of moral realism, the belief in objective moral absolutes out there. The thing out there that faith clings to, and that underwrites our moral judgements, functions to give people a kind of cosmic legitimation that they crave more than anything, that they have always had, and which they will not give up freely.

Our discussion so far indicates what Nietzsche meant by using the phrase 'beyond good and evil'. He rightly thought that our moral discourse is full of false beliefs, illusions, awkward leftovers from the past, and dirty tricks. Morality is, very often, not something ultimate in our lives, but a fig leaf; a tool in our power games, as the playwright Bernard Shaw used to say so clearly through his plays. That is why the whole subject of moral philosophy has become a morass, so difficult that it is one of the least-developed and most obscure territories in the whole of philosophy. Only a handful of philosophers have ever succeeded in making any significant contribution to it at all. (I'd say Aristotle, Spinoza, Bentham, Hegel, Nietzsche and Foucault, but I'm probably asking for trouble.) By urging us to take up a standpoint 'beyond good and evil', Nietzsche is saying that we should look at the various competing human moralities as if from outside, and in a cool and critical spirit. We should question the morality of morality. What good does it do? Will these teachings really help us to conduct our common life more successfully? Does our morality really succeed in making our life seem to us more worthwhile?

Good questions; and they are the reason why over the past decades I have tried– rather intermittently, I confess – to work out a moral philosophy of my own that gives answers to them. I'll give a very brief sketch of a few of my ideas, and you may find them very odd: but you must remember that I find all the more orthodox moralities and justifications of morality to be unbearably obscure, and often repulsive. I have felt that I must be as radical in ethics as I notoriously am in doctrine. Sorry!

Before sketching my own ideas about how we should see morality, I must briefly mention a second large background fact. Moral discourse in our tradition has not only been heavily influenced by legal metaphors; it has also been much influenced by Jewish and Christian apocalyptic myths, which have pictured the world and our life in terms of a cosmic struggle between the Principles of Good and Evil. The Christian was a soldier, and the Church on earth was 'Militant'. (It was 'Expectant' in Purgatory and, as we saw earlier, 'Triumphant' in Heaven.) The persistence of this mythology still to this day encourages moral realism and moral dualism, as when people focus upon an Evil Empire out there, an enemy to confront that gives purpose to their lives. 'We are the good people, who with God's help will struggle against this evil Power, and will prevail.' But what we observers notice is that where this style of thinking is influential morality tends to be led by an urgent (and very expensive) quest to identify, hunt down and destroy 'evil'. Reactive, negative emotions become very prominent, and the typical moralist is the crusader, the witch-hunter, the purity campaigner, and the embittered victim.

My own account, as you will soon see, does not contain anything of that kind, because I have been attempting to describe a purely affirmative ethics of value that simply does without ideas of sin, evil, warfare, punishment, vindication and so on. I have felt that above all I must try to cut out of my ethics all the stuff that poisons the soul.[3]

---

3 In what follows I draw upon ideas first put forward in *The New Christian Ethics*, London: SCM Press, 1987. Notice that I make ethics thoroughly subjective and emotive. We, and we only, put the values into life by the ways in which we feel about things.

Why? Because modern ethics is no longer a struggle to appear righteous in the eyes of one's neighbours, and no longer a cosmic battle against evil supernatural Powers. It is first and foremost a struggle for *value*, a struggle against nihilism, a struggle against the pervasive feeling that our life is worthless, meaningless, brief and insignificant. The first task of ethics today is to make life feel worth living.

Our ethics then must be rooted in our own being as biological organisms who are perpetually appetitive, questing, with a strong appetite for experience and an urgent interest in life. In us emotion flows all the time, and reacts at once and very sensitively to everything we come across. We are not pure *thinkers* at all: on the contrary, our first response to each thing is a very delicately attuned feeling response, favourable or unfavourable. We may call this response an *evaluation*, because I am suggesting that all our experience is coloured by our likes and dislikes, by extremely varied and delicately adjusted feelings. And when language enters; when we classify and interpret our experience by putting it into words – *then* our primitive feeling responses to experience are carried over into our language, and every description of things and events carries with it some evaluative overtones, tilting our sympathy one way or the other.

Now, our language includes a sort of inventory of our world. All the kinds of experience, processes, situations and things that together make up our life-world are duly represented in our language. And because the ways we instinctively and immediately feel about everything come to be associated with and to flavour all our words, our language not only contains a comprehensive evaluation of our life as we presently experience it, but also, because it is our inherited language, our language tends to teach us our culture – a culture being an inherited traditional evaluation of life. The flavours annexed to words suggest to us how we should behave towards everything we come across.

Does this mean that our culture – that is, our inherited language – pre-programmes us to respond to, to evaluate, and to treat everything exactly as it prescribes? No, not at all, for because we are ourselves living and changing beings, we are always slightly modifying our received language, and therewith also adjusting our received valuations of things, as we go along. Thus our language is our culture, and is our overall evaluation of life. As we learn it, it shapes our feelings and helps us to build and to colour up our common world. But our feeling life is not mechanical and automatic: we are living beings, always changing, and we never exactly repeat the previous generation's world view, feelings and way of life. On the contrary, our culture, our language, our feeling life, *and the world itself*, are all *transactional*; that is, they are being renegotiated and evolving every day. In life, everything changes a little all the time – and we are part of it all.

Thus our language gives us a choice. We may accept and go along with the received current evaluations of things, and so fit in with and accept the conventional wisdom. But it quite often happens that we disagree with the current evaluation of something that is coded into the way it is currently spoken of. We feel that it has been unjustly given a bad name. It is underestimated. In which case, we can argue for a change in the vocabulary that is used to describe that thing. During the 1960s, as people first realized all these points, there were successful campaigns to alter somewhat the vocabulary in which we all of us habitually spoke of – and therefore acted towards – women, homosexual men, black people and many other groups who had long been linguistically stigmatized. And mention of the 1960s reminds me that it was indeed during that period that we all of us gradually learnt to think about morality in the new way that I am describing – that is as human, as transactional, as embedded in language, and as changeable by consent, through public debate and linguistic change.

This new way of thinking about ethics is anti-realist, for it makes ethics human, and grounds it in our flickering and ever-changing life of feeling. Nothing in ethics needs to be thought of as 'absolute' or as 'eternal': on the contrary, everything in ethics is immanent, human and in principle revisable. All of which shows us that we have found here our answer to the problem of nihilism. Ever since the days of Galileo and Descartes it has been thought that orthodox scientific method is by far the best and most powerful way to knowledge that human beings have ever devised – and that it pictures the Universe as a value-free zone, a huge, dead machine with no immanent purposiveness at all. From Pascal onwards people complained of feeling threatened by nihilism, until eventually Nietzsche announced its arrival. For him – for Nietzsche, that is – the end of moral realism is the decisive point. We now know that 'the moral interpretation of the world' was an illusion. There is no hidden force for good secretly at work out there. We are alone. Nobody cares; and when we become extinct – which we now fear may actually happen within a couple of centuries or less – the Universe won't even notice our absence.

The new ethical theory that I have been describing proposes an answer to all this. True, the world view of natural science is value-neutral; but the human life-world, which for us is *our* world and the primary world, is steeped in evaluations. An evaluation is a human feeling response of liking or dislike. Everything has a value colouration of one sort or another, and we humans in the world of everyday life are constantly comparing and sharing our valuations of things.

To see how nihilism is conquered in everyday life, let us continue the exposition of our post-1960s ethics of value creation.

The fear that our whole life is ultimately meaningless and worthless is partly based, as we have seen, on the belief that science is by far the best way to knowledge we've got, coupled with the fact that the scientific world-picture does not find any purposiveness or values in the world. But there is also the fact that the Augustinian Christianity which was dominant among both Catholics and Protestants until the late seventeenth century took such a very gloomy view of human nature and of this world. In retrospect, it was horrible. It located almost all goodness, beauty and happiness in the eternal world, and portrayed our ordinary human life as utterly wretched. When people began to lose faith in the eternal world, they had nothing left but what the Book of Common Prayer (1662) describes as 'the miseries of this sinful world' – that is, nihilism; for we can now see that nihilism is an artificial bogey, something that was constructed by Augustinian

Christianity in order to frighten us into holding on to realistic theism and supernatural faith.

> . . . always keep hold of nurse
> For fear of finding something worse.

So during the early modern period – roughly, the period of our Tudor monarchs – we inherited from the Middle Ages a life-world that looked rather shabby and dismal. Since then there has been a long, hard struggle to upgrade the life-world, and learn how to enjoy life. We have struggled to redeem the world and this life by slowly revaluing and upgrading (for example) time, matter, the body, Nature, the senses, the emotions, women and human love. And it is against this background that I formulate my version of the moral task. For the sake of the general happiness, we should teach people to value every aspect of the body, this life, each person, and this world as highly as is self-consistently possible. We should try to be generous, and should do as little denouncing, condemning, disparaging and judging as we can. We should look at what the study of natural history, for example, has done to differentiate, diversify and enrich the perceived natural world, and should do likewise. The life-world is maximally enriched and beautified for all if each individual does her bit to love and care for her own corner of it. Individually and collectively, we are all of us happier when we value life and the life-world highly, so it is rational to pursue as life-affirming an ethical policy as possible.

In our world a very great number of people consider themselves to be members of badly treated minorities. Such people seem to devote much of their time to brooding over ancient wrongs, and nourishing grudges, grievances and dreams of bloody revenge. To do this poisons the soul, and to such people I say: 'Leave your ethnic group, your victimized minority! Leave them! The true conquest of evil and nihilism is simply the practice of magnanimity. Try to be as consistently affirmative as possible, and try to avoid any complaining. Do not get into disputes, or seek compensation. Instead, just try to cherish and enrich your corner of the world, and so contribute something to the whole human scene. Create value! Value is saving Grace!'

This may seem a very simple-minded and thin injunction, but you must remember that I am a non-realist. We, and only we, have the responsibly for building our world, and making our own lives seem to us to be meaningful and valuable. The world as such, and independently of us, does not contain any ready-made, pre-existent moral facts, and does not prescribe any ready-made ethical theory to us. In the matter of ethics, we are not *given* anything. There is no divinely revealed moral code, the physical universe does not have any natural moral law built into it, and our conscience is a cultural creation which is not at all a reliable moral guide. There are no ready-made human rights or absolute obligations that just present themselves to us. The moral order is not a ready-made, intelligible system out there, which we are predesigned to live in. On the contrary, I am suggesting that *we* invented all the strange jumble of moral theories that we have inherited, and I say that most of them are not very good. So I am proposing only a very liberal moral theory that says that it is rational for us all to pick out and follow practices that will enhance our life's perceived value and our overall enjoyment of it. To that end we should all love life and try to live it to the full – which is what ordinary language nowadays recommends to us. We should try to raise the value of our own corner of the world by making a habit of avoiding the negative emotions – *ressentiment*[4] and so on – and cultivating as generous and affirmative an outlook as we can. This will involve valuing each person and each aspect of the world and of our life as highly as is self-consistently possible. Then, leave it at that. Don't discuss sin: forget the word. Just get on with redeeming the world, by revaluing it.

This is a very general prescription, and people may carry it out in a great variety of different ways. But then, I have sought to avoid any picture of morality as a standard, one-size-fits-all burden of duties, commandments and prohibitions, to be imposed upon everybody alike. On the contrary, I have borne in mind the

---

4 Nietzsche's word, used by him to epitomize the 'reactive' emotions.

great diversity of modern people and modern society. I have argued that we should see morality in the age of nihilism as a creative, productive task, the task of creating value and making life precious and happy for all. This is a task which people can discharge in a great variety of ways through their jobs, their hobbies, their loves and so on. The emphasis is upon value-creation and diversification. In the age of nihilism we do best to see the task of religion and morality as being *celebratory*, and like *art*.

A last point. My account has been rather unsystematic, and I see that Nigel Leaves, in his recent book, describes me as having had about five worthwhile ideas about ethics this last thirty or forty years, without ever developing much of a system. That is, I don't really succeed in unifying either the moral order itself, or the human moral life, in quite the way that Plato taught us to expect.

I think I can't apologize for this, because in my view we did not appear on earth to find a ready-made moral order waiting for us, like a house to be lived in. On the contrary, human beings have had to start from scratch. We have produced many moralities, and we have made many attempts to codify them. But today our received moral traditions look a bit of a muddle. Nothing guarantees that a convincing and coherent account of the moral order is just sitting out there waiting for someone to come along and spell it out. And although most of us would like to have a reasonably coherent and consistent moral life-policy and form of selfhood, nothing guarantees that a fully unified and saintly human selfhood is ever going to be achievable. We are not given any ready-made unity of all values, or of all the virtues. The best we can do is to raise our own spirits by doing what we can do to inject enough meaning and value into life to make the world beautiful and life worth living.

It follows that – like George Eliot, I think[5] – I have to admit that we can't aim quite as high as the saints in the past. But I can claim that something very good and worthwhile remains within reach.

---

5 In her preface to *Middlemarch*, 1872.